On Low Ground,

Lower Ground

在低处,
更低处

On Low Ground,
Lower Ground

在低处，
更低处

Long Quan

龙泉

Translated by Ouyang Yu

译者：欧阳昱

PUNCHER & WATTMANN

© Long Quan 2019

Cover image: Zhao Baokang

First published in 2019

Published by Puncher and Wattmann

PO Box 279

Waratah NSW 2298

Australia

http://www.puncherandwattmann.com

puncherandwattmann@bigpond.com

ISBN 9781925780215

NATIONAL
LIBRARY
OF AUSTRALIA

A catalogue record for this book is available from the National Library of Australia

Contents

在低处，更低处

我一直往低处看
往最低最低处看
城市以下的低处
楼房以下的低处
炊烟以下的低处
在低处，寻找住所

我一直往低处看
往最低最低处看
阳光以下的低处
泥土以下的低处
种子以下的低处
在低处，寻找果实

我一直往低处看
往最低最低处看
目光所及的低处
芸芸众生的低处
在低处，更低处
寻找幸福的泉眼

On Low Ground, Lower Ground

I have been looking at the low ground
the lowest ground, ever
the low ground under the city
the buildings
and the smoke from the kitchen chimneys
seeking a residence on low ground

I have been looking at the low ground
the lowest ground, ever
the low ground under the sunlight
the soil
and the seeds
seeking fruit on low ground

I have been looking at the low ground
the lowest ground, ever
the low ground my eye hits
the low ground of the masses
on low ground, lower ground
seeking the mouth, of a spring

画瓷像的人

快要死的人
已经死去的人
在你这里排队等候
你专门为他们画像
用光滑的瓷板
画出深刻的岁月
生意的好坏，取决于
能否把死人画得更像
眼睛是否更有神……
闲暇时，你也画些风景
画些花鸟虫鱼，而现在
一个画家的梦，只能
在死人身上延续

The Man Who Does the Porcelain Portraits

the dead

or those about to die

are queuing up here for you

as you are doing their portraits on porcelain

creating deep years

on smooth porcelain plates

a good business depends

on whether you can achieve the likeness of the dead

or do their eyes in a way that they come alive...

in your freer time, you also do landscape

with flowers, birds, insects and fish, but now

the dream of an artist could only be continued

amongst the dead

读高二的女儿

女儿在柔和的灯光下安然入睡
没有做完的作业、试卷以及
甜甜的梦洒落一地
她忘了关灯就睡着了
她来不及关灯就睡着了
睡着了是很自然的事情
睡着了是很快乐的事情
在这午夜凌乱的时刻
女儿进入甜甜的梦境
十六岁的快乐在梦中出现

My Year 11 Daughter

she fell asleep in the soft lamplight

the floor strewn with unfinished homework

exam papers and sweet dreams

she had fallen asleep before she could switch off the lights

before she had time to do so

it's natural to fall asleep

it's a pleasure to fall asleep

in this messy midnight moment

my daughter had entered into a sweet dream

her 16-year-old happiness appearing in it

一条仇恨的标语

一条充满仇恨的标语
在这个村庄隐匿了几十年
在一个角落，它褪去了时间的外衣
它的仇恨从牙缝里挤出
尖锐的牙齿已完全脱落
一些若隐若现的伤痛
被写进青砖的皱纹，一群农民
怎么会藏有哪么多的炸药
并以最恶毒的语言形式
投向一个从不认识的人——
那些不满，它自己都莫名其妙
火药味伴着干燥的牛粪
在岁月的尘埃中消失
一条仇恨的标语，也在
风雨侵蚀中自然死亡

A Hate Slogan

a slogan, filled with hatred

has been in hiding in this village for decades

in a corner, it has stripped itself off time's garments

the hatred squeezed from between its teeth

all its sharp teeth fallen in their entirety

traces of pain, half visible

having been written

into the wrinkles of the black bricks. but how can a group of peasants

have hidden so many dynamites

and, with the foulest language

hurtled them towards a total stranger—

the discontent bewildered even by itself

the smell of the dynamite, accompanied with the dry cow dung

has since disappeared, in the dust of the years

a hate slogan, too

has died its natural death, in the erosion of wind and rain

那一片荒地

父亲走了，母亲也跟着走了
留下一栋老屋，以及离老屋
几百米远的一块荒地，那块荒地
曾经种满红薯，曾经盛满油菜花的芬芳
那块长满荆丛被岁月遗弃的荒地
为父亲漂泊的一生打上了句号
让他与生养他的土地如此亲近
让他与至亲的人形影不离
有一次，我看见落日的余晖
洒在父亲七十多岁的脸上
和母亲微微弯曲的后背
那熠熠生辉的一瞬，放大了
父母一生的幸福，而这种时光
只有那么几年，他们把自己的夕阳
寄存在那片荒地，和那些植物的根茎

The Patch of Wasteland

Father left; Mother followed also

leaving behind an old house and a patch of wasteland

hundreds of metres away from the house, where

Father had grown sweet potatoes and rape with fragrant flowers

the patch, deserted by the years and overgrown with clusters of brambles

had put a period to Father's drifting life

enabling him to keep close to the land where he was born and bred

like a shadow that never left his loved ones

on one occasion, I saw the afterglow

on his face of 70-odd years

and Mother's back, slightly bent

the shining instant enlarged

the happiness of their life, and that instant

lasted only a few years and, now, they have kept their setting sun

in the patch, along with the roots of those plants

与妻书

你唠叨
我把你当母亲
你撒娇
我把你当女儿
你大度
我把你当姐姐
你任性
我把你当妹妹
你批评我
我把你当领导
你帮助我
我把你当老师
你鼓励我
我把你当朋友
你鞭策我
我把你当同事
你疼我，爱我，包容我
——你是我老婆

Letter to My Wife

you nag

and I regard you as Mother

you play the woman

and I regard you as Daughter

you are generous

and I regard you as Older Sister

you are childish

and I regard you as Younger Sister

you criticise me

and I regard you as my superior

you help me

and I regard you as my teacher

you encourage me

and I regard you as a friend

you urge me on

and I regard you as a colleague

you soft-spot me, you love me and you tolerate me

—you are my wife

纯度:99.99%的金黄

秋天的田野一片金黄
那是我喜欢的颜色
那是阳光和汗水淬火后的结晶

父亲说过，黄土里能长出黄金
那时的我一脸茫然一脸疑惑
他在黄土地里一辈子两手空空

那随风起伏的金黄
是父亲一生的缩影
从这片黄土地走出的五个子女
是这方圆几十里最好的收成

一粒太阳洒下一片金黄
一粒金黄需要一千粒汗水
纯度百分之九十九点九九的金黄
是父亲一生寄予的希望

Purity: 99.99% of Gold

the fields in autumn were a spread of gold
a colour I like
a crystallisation of sunlight and sweat, both hardened

according to Father, gold could grow out of the yellow earth
I looked unconvinced when he made that remark
as he remained empty-handed, having worked all his life on the yellow
       earth

the gold, undulating with the wind
was his life in miniature
his five kids, both boys and girls
were the best harvest within miles

a grain of the sun sprayed a spread of gold
and a grain of gold would need a thousand drops of sweat
gold, its purity 99.99%
was the hope Father had had all his life

坐在云端上的二伯父

拖拉机突突突一路高歌

在一条直线上一路高歌

在一种声音里一路高歌

它满载着丰收的稻谷和喜悦

二伯父坐在高高的谷堆上

比拖拉机高出几米

仿佛坐在云端里

这一年我十二岁

小学刚刚毕业

他请我当账房先生

让我坐在驾驶室里

给我买糖水冰棒，请我下馆子

看着我，像看着家族的希望

沉默寡言的二伯父，一辈子抽旱烟

喜欢听收音机里的"三国"

点子多，力气轻，肯帮人

唯一的缺点就是不识字

如今，坐在云端上的二伯父

还在看着我，他的模样一点没变

他看我的样子一点没变

My Paternal Uncle the Second, Sitting in a Cloud

the tractor was singing, chugging all the way

along a straight line

and in one voice

carrying a bumper crop of rice and delight

sitting on the stack, Uncle the Second was

taller than the tractor by two metres

as if sitting in a cloud

that year, I was twelve

having just graduated from the primary school

he invited me to be his accountant

by getting me to sit in his cabin

buying me sweet popsicles and treating me to dinner in a restaurant

and looked at me as if looking at someone as the hope of the Family

the quiet Uncle the Second had smoked tobacco, in a long-stemmed pipe,
      all his life

and he liked listening to *The Three States* on radio

he got lots of ideas, didn't have much physical strength but was ready to
      help

except that he was illiterate

now, Uncle the Second, sitting in a cloud

is still looking down at me, his features unchanged

and the way he looks at me remains unchanged in the least

春天的一幅草图

一张陷入泥土深处的犁

一件披在稻草人身上的蓑衣

一头在斗牛场勇猛病态的牛

一个缺席的老实本分的农夫

一道来自城市森林布谷鸟的指令

一声来自天国的婉转哨音

在这样一幅潦草的图画中

春天悄然潜入……

The Drawing of a Spring

a plough, stuck deep in the soil

a straw rain cape, on a scarecrow

a sick bull that had been brave in a bullring

a peasant, honest and dutiful, who was absent

an order issued by a cuckoo in a city forest

a whistle from the heavenly kingdom

the spring has quietly seeped in

in this scribbly drawing...

平衡术

向左一点，向右一点
快一点，慢一点，更爱一点，不爱一点
重一点，轻一点，肉麻一点，绅士一点
大一点，小一点，阳光一点，阴暗一点
深一点，浅一点，调皮一点，木讷一点
多一点，少一点，撒娇一点，严肃一点
好一点，坏一点，淫荡一点，正经一点
涨一点，跌一点，滥情一点，专一一点
急一点，缓一点，极端一点，隐忍一点，
白一点，黑一点，完美一点，个性一点
甜一点，苦一点，善良一点，不善良一点
长一点，短一点，喜欢一点，不喜欢一点
胖一点，瘦一点，笑一点，不笑一点……
这一点，一点
让许多人失去重心失去平衡
我又一次走在独木桥上
身体内部摇摇晃晃——
世界与自我失去平衡，心乱一点
灵魂与肉体失去平衡，轻飘一点
左手与右手失去平衡，倾斜一点

眼睛与嘴巴失去平衡，结巴一点
这一点，一点
让我止步不前
让我心惊胆战
让我忽然站立不动
——冷静一点，清醒一点！

The Balancing Act

slightly to the left or slightly to the right

faster or slower; love more or love less

heavier or lighter; be less gentlemanly or be it more

bigger or smaller; sun-shinier or darker

deeper or shallower; naughtier or woodener

give more or give less; act more spoiled or more serious

be better or badder; obscener or decenter

swell up more or fall further; be more sentimental or more focused

be rasher or more relaxed; be more extreme or more patient

whiter or blacker; more perfect or more individualistic

sweeter or bitterer; kinder-hearted or less kind

longer or shorter; like it more or like it less

fatter or thinner; smile more or smile less

more, or, less

it's just this that has caused most to lose their balance

once again I walk the one-wood bridge

swaying from side to side in the heart of my hearts—

the world and I have lost balance, my heart confused

the soul and the body have lost balance, becoming lighter

my left hand and my right have lost balance, slightly inclined

my eyes and my mouth have lost balance, stammering a little

more, or, less

it's just this that has stopped me in my tracks

frightening me

till I come to a standstill

—calm down! Wake up!

母子图

在黄昏的河边
在大自然的怀抱
一头母牛和它的小牛犊
悠游在天地之间，自由自在
它们那么渺小，又那么高大
她蹲下身子，拍下母子情深
母亲躺开胸怀给幼崽喂奶
夕阳西下，远山近水作为背景
哦，来一张，再来一张……
天高云远，河流曲折，岁月悠长
母牛慈祥惶惑而神秘地看着她
她们的眼神在交流的瞬间
流露出同样的母性——
满足，欣喜而又安静

Portrait of a Mother and Her Son

a riverbank at dusk

a cow and a calf

in the arms of Nature

were wandering, at ease, between heaven and earth

they were at once small and huge

she squatted on her haunches, a picture of motherly love

baring her breast to suckle her baby

under the setting sun and against the background of far mountains and
near waters

oh, a picture, then another—

the sky high and the clouds faraway, the river meandering and the years
long

the cow, benign and bewildered, threw a mysterious look at her

in the moment in which they exchanged a look

they revealed the same sense of motherhood—

content, with peace and quiet

最后一个要求

追悼会前几天
他提出最后一个要求
比他年长的不要来
年轻的可以来
比他官大的不要来
官小的可以来
比他有钱的不要来
钱少的可以来
比他活得好的不要来
不好的可以来
结果，那天来的人很少
他躺在水晶棺里
眼睛一直没有闭上
几滴浑浊的泪水，在
　　　　眼
　　　　角
　　　　挂
　　　　着

His Final Request

a few days before the funeral

he made his last request

that no one older than him may come

but that anyone younger may

that no one in a higher position than his may come

but that anyone in a lower may

that no one richer than him may come

but that anyone less rich may

and that no one better-off than him may come

but that anyone less well-off may

as a result, few turned up that day

lying in his crystal coffin, he

didn't close his eyes

a few muddy teardrops were hanging

          on

          the

          corner

          of

          his

          eyes

结

一棵树上有很多的结

我爬一段解开一个，爬一段解开一个

解眉头的结

解心头的结

解肚脐眼上的结中结

不用利爪，不用牙咬

用心，用生命的灰烬

解开众多的纠结

让这棵树腰杆挺直，拥有

健康的生活，完美的爱情，顶天立地的事业

拥有更多的风，雨，雷，电……

The Knots

a tree had many a knot

as I climbed up one section after another of it I untied one knot after

      another

the knot of brows

the knot of hearts

the knot of knots on the navel

not with my claws or my teeth

but with my heart, and with the ashes of my life

untying a mass of knots

so that the tree might straighten up, to possess

a healthy life, a perfect love and a sky-holding career

and to possess more wind, more rain, more thunder and more lightning...

半个我

老师说我，上课不够用心
前一段还可以，后一段只有半个我在听
领导指出，如果你工作能100%投入
你的人生将比现在精彩几倍
妻子说，你每天早出晚归
有时几天不回。是不是也在提醒
只有半个我在跟她一起生活
这半个我，让我胆寒心惊
那幽灵一样飘荡的另一半
在哪里？是不是一直附在我的体内
跟你在一起，一直盯着你看的那个人
和你说话，一起走在阳光下的那个人
与你肌肤相亲灵魂相吻的那个人
是不是也只是半个我？半个我
神出鬼没，多么可怕的事实
半个我，多么真切的存在
它游离体外，又深入骨髓
和我一起，一生一世逍遥自在

Half of Me

my teacher said that I wasn't attentive enough in class
I was okay with the first part of it but, in the next part, only half of me
     was listening
my boss said that my life could have been much better
if I had put 100% of my energy in it
my wife said that I went out in the morning and came back in the evening
sometimes not coming home for days. Did she suggest
that only half of me is living with her?
this half of me scares me
but where is the other half
drifting like a ghost? Is it the guy, adhering to the insides of me
who has been gazing at you?
the guy, talking with you, who has been walking in the sun?
the guy, close to your skin, whose soul has been kissing yours?
is it also only half of me? The half of me
comes and goes, like a shadow, a terrifying fact
but half of me is a real existence
drifting outside my body but deep inside my bone marrow
accompanying me for life, leisurely and carefree

红苹果

我看着她
她看着我
我们保持了适度的距离和礼节
不知不觉中，尘埃落定
风雨都在窗外
她长了皱纹
我添了白发

The Red Apple

I look at her
as she looks at me
we keep a proper distance and etiquette
before we realise it, the dust has settled
the wind and rain kept outside the windows
she has grown wrinkles
and I, grey hair

慢

我想把速度降下来
把生活的节奏降下来
降下来，就像一列高速行驶的列车
快要进站。就像一场音乐会
接近尾声。就像一阵雨
由急促到舒缓
降下来，在慢的节奏里
周围的世界理智、冷静
降下来，在正常的速度里
慢慢找回自己

Slow

I'd like to speed down
to slow the rhythm of life
like a fast-travelling train
about to enter into the station, like a concert
about to draw to a close, like a rain
moving from rapidity to slowness
so that, in the rhythm of slowness
the surrounding world becomes more reasonable and calmer
and, in the normal speed
I can find myself back

付小明杂货店

高中同学付小明
他在小镇开了一间杂货店
做点小生意维持生计
他卖锄头、扫把和簸箕
也卖电线、插座和小电器
读书时跟我同桌
喜欢摆弄钢笔、铅笔
和橡皮擦，他机灵、调皮
英语课上打瞌睡
我想买点什么，不知道
家里的拖把是否要更换
风扇在夏天是否还能转
付小明微笑的脸
始终如一。他告诉我
杂货店开了二十年
店名是英语老师题写的
说到刚刚去世的周老师
付小明语调哽咽……
我们提到很多同学的名字

有的经常光顾他的小店
有一些变得非常遥远陌生

Fu Xiaoming's Grocery Store

Fu Xiaoming, a classmate of mine in senior middle school
was running a grocery store in town
engaging in small business to make ends meet
selling hoes, brooms and dustpans
selling, too, electrical wires, plugs and small electrical appliances
at school, he was my desk-mate
and liked toying with pens, pencils
and erasers. A sharp and naughty boy
he used to doze off in English classes
I'd like to buy something there, not sure
if I'd need to replace my broom
or if my electrical fan would continue to work in summer
but Fu Xiaoming kept a smiling face
as always. He told me
that he had been running this shop for the last twenty years
the name of his shop was hand-written by his English teacher
as he talked about Mr Zhou, the teacher, who had just died
Fu Xiaoming sobbed...
we mentioned many of the names of our classmates

some would often visit his shop

while others had grown distant and strange

刺

那些过去的事
有时像根刺
扎进肉里，扎进心里
轻轻拨出时
比扎进时
更痛

The Thorn

those things of the past

like a thorn

sometimes prick into the flesh, the heart

when you gently pull it out

it hurts more

than when it pricks in

桥

水干涸了
路改道了
它的功能失去了
只能守着车水马龙的记忆
安度晚年

The Bridge

the water has dried up
and the route has changed its course
with its function lost
the bridge spends its evening years in peace and quiet
keeping alive the memory of the bygone traffic

声音收集者

在静夜。

我听见"滴答""滴答"闹钟的声音

水龙头漏水的声音，蟑螂吃西瓜的声音

苍蝇咬鸡蛋的声音，蚊子吸血的声音

墙上壁虎的声音，公园里老猫叫春的声音

狐狸发出饥饿而阴森的声音

猪被杀了两刀到处乱跑的声音

狗失去主人哀鸣的声音

猴子在花果山嬉闹的声音

马在夜草原仰首嘶鸣的声音

公鸡打鸣母鸡下蛋的声音

老鼠在房梁上窃喜的声音

小猫在夜色中蹑手蹑脚的声音

有人"咚咚咚"上楼的声音……

在静夜。

我听见"吱吱""吱吱"蟋蟀的声音

雄鸟与雌鸟交配的声音

树与藤交劲而眠的声音

远处波涛撞击堤岸的声音

汽车相撞飞机坠崖"隆隆"的声音
建筑工地打桩机"夯夯"的声音
8.8级地震地动山摇的声音
泥石流轰然冲倒房屋的声音
凄厉的北风刺向破旧门窗的声音
冰与火相克的声音
嫩芽破土而出的声音
雨打在心上和地上的声音
雷电击倒一堵墙又压着一个人的声音
男人与女人永无休止爱恨交织的声音……

在静夜。
我听见神从天国发出的声音
太阳居高临下又俯首称臣的声音
月光照亮人间黑暗和丑陋的声音
布道者虔诚的声音，背叛者忏悔的声音
哲学家形而上的声音，农民工形而下的声音
生命在血管里流动的声音
命运在高速路上激烈碰撞的声音
智者乐呵呵的声音，白痴哼哈哈的声音
流行歌手从颤抖的皮肤上发出的声音
诗人从灵魂里发出的声音……

这些声音来自夜晚和白天
这些声音来自交融和碰撞
这些声音来自地狱和天国
我把这些声音收集起来
作为我死而复生的筹码
把它翻译成简单的现代汉语
打通宇宙与人类的秘密通道

A Collector of Sounds

on a still night

I heard the tick-tock of an alarm clock

the drip-drip-drip of a tap, the sound of a cockroach eating into a
watermelon

the biting of a fly on an egg or that of a mosquito sucking the blood

the sound of a wall tiger (gecko) or the crying spring (catawauling) of an
old cat in the park

the sound, hungry and sinister, of a fox

the wild running around of a pig, hacked twice

the whimpering of a dog, having lost its master

the capering of monkeys in the Flower and Fruit Mountain

the neighing of a horse on the grassland, its head raised

the crowing of a cock and a hen laying its egg

the merrymaking of a rat on the beam

the tiptoeing of a tiny cat at night

and the stomping of someone going upstairs...

on a still night

I heard the chirping of the crickets

the mating of a male bird with a female

the sleeping of a tree with a vine

the hitting of distant waves against the embankment

the collision of a car or the crashing of an airplane off a cliff the ramming of pile drivers on a construction site

the shaking of mountains by an earthquake measuring 8.8 on the Richter
  Scale

the rushing off of houses in a mudslide

the piercing of old doors or windows by a bleak northerly wind

the overcoming of each other by ice and fire

the breaking out of earth by the tender buds

the hitting of the rain on the heart and the soil

the thunderstorm felling a wall that buries someone

the interweaving of love and hatred between man and woman...

on a still night

I heard the sound issued by God from the heavenly kingdom

the bowing of the sun even as it overrules everything

the shining of the moonlight over the dark and the ugly

the pious prayer of the sermoniser and the confessions of a betrayer

the metaphysical voice of a philosopher or the paraphysical voice of a
  peasant

the running of life in the veins

the fierce collision of fates on the freeway

the cheerfulness of the wise and the whooping of the idiotic

the singing of a pop singer, issued from the tremulous skin

the voice of a poet from his soul...

these sounds come from day and night

they come from mergings and collisions

and from hell and heaven

I collect them as chips for my return to life

I translate them into the simplest Chinese words

to connect the secret passage to mankind and the universe

双面人

我是一个隐姓埋名者

我有过许多笔名、假名、曾用名

我戴过一个又一个很多的面具

我的快乐和痛苦不轻易流露

我的英俊和丑陋你看不到

我是武士佩剑，骑士风流

我是文人和商人的杂种

我是荣光的白天和屈辱的夜晚

我是高尚和粗俗的怪胎

我是男女不分的人妖

我是功名和利禄的孪生兄弟

我是清高和不屑的金色种子

我是热烈而盲目的黄玫瑰

我是忧郁而浪漫的薰衣草

我是情欲泛滥的梦魇

我是爱情专一的国王

我是等待打开的密码

我是已经解开的心结

我演的角色自然而真实

没有主角和配角
没有灯光和舞台

The Double-Faced Man

a concealer of my own identity
I have used many different pennames, pseudonyms, and alias
and I have put on one mask after another
never do I easily reveal my happiness or pain
and I render my handsomeness or ugliness invisible to any
I'm a warrior with a sword, a womanising knight
a hybrid business man of letters
a day of glory and a night of shame
a freak combining the sublime and the vulgar
a monster both male and female
a twin brother of fame and fortune
a golden seed of aloof and distain
a yellow rose of passion and blindness
a lavender of sorrow and romance
a nightmare of overflowing desire
a king of dedicated love
a code waiting to be decoded
a heart knot unknotted
I play a role natural and real

without the lead role or supporting roles

without the lights or the stage

8月17日的稻田

这一刻
我俯瞰熟悉的南方稻田
奶奶的织布机
仍在不停地转动
只是颜色由黑而白
由白而绿——深绿
一幅几十万米的长卷
镌刻在祖国的一枚纽扣上

The Rice Paddy on August 17

in that moment
I looked at the familiar southern rice paddies
as Grandma's loom
kept working
except that the colour turned from black to white
and from white to green—a dark green
a scroll, hundreds of thousands of metres long
engraved on a button of the motherland

跟着火车跑

我一直想写写火车
写写跟着火车跑的感觉
它对天长鸣的汽笛就是我内心的呐喊
它擒住双轨的轮子就是我不知疲惫的双腿
它拥挤不堪的人流就是我南来北往的欲望
它茫然丢下的垃圾就是我写下的愤怒的诗句
它在丘陵中穿行预示我人生曲折命运的坎坷
它在平原上疾驰表明我视野开阔前途一片光明
它进出一个又一个隧道就是我一次又一次历险
它出站时长啸，进站时呜咽……
此时，许多人已经沉沉睡去
而我还有跑的感觉

Running with the Train

I have always wanted to write about the train

about how I feel when running with it

its whistling in the air a cry out loud from my heart

its wheels clutching the rails my tireless feet

its overcrowded people my desire to go north and south

its chucked rubbish my angry lines

its traversing through the hills my life journey of ups and downs

its dash across the plain the widening of my field of vision with a bright
      future

its going through tunnels my adventures

it howls when departing from the station and sobs when entering it...

by now, many have gone asleep

and I still have that feeling, of running

进站

挂在墙上的钟
是一个象征
它俯瞰大厅发生的一切
来来往往的人，或从容，或焦躁
或沉默不语，或滔滔不绝
站在这里，你就像站在河边
人流如水流，湍急或舒缓
清澈或浑浊，都在一个拐点转换
不必感慨逝者如斯，人生不易
你所担心的，时间会解决
你所忽视的，神在关注
在平凡的生活中
谁能卷起惊涛骇浪
谁能梳理万般愁绪
墙上的钟，滴答滴答
它提醒你：该进站了

Entering into a Station

the clock on the wall
is a symbol
overlooking everything that is happening in the hall
the people, coming and going, are relaxed or fidgety
they talk or keep silence
standing here, you feel as if you were standing by the river
the flow of people resembles the water, torrential or leisurely
clean or turbulent, all in transit at one turning point
one doesn't have to worry about their passage; life is not easy
time will solve whatever that worries you
God pays attention to whatever you have overlooked
in an ordinary life
who can keep up tempestuous waves
and who can sort out moods of all sorts
the clock on the wall, tick-tocking
reminds you that it's time to enter the station

一件旧物

它来我家好几年了吧
在一个角落
不曾引人注意，似乎
也不曾派过什么用场
它占据了一块地盘
有时显得碍手碍脚
局促，委琐，灰头土脸
与周围环境格格不入
被人漠视和无用的痛苦
伴它无数个夜晚和白昼
有一天，它忽然不见了
妻说，被收废品的人拿走了
五块钱算是搬运的费用
这让我想起一个人
他来到人世短暂的光阴里
不曾留下任何痕迹
不曾让人记住一点好处
他走的时候又
总会有人要来送送

An Old Item

it's been in my house for several years already
in a corner
that has drawn no attention nor has it been
put to any use
taking up space
standing in the way, sometimes
uneasy, abject and dust-covered
at odds with its surroundings
accompanied, for days and nights, with its pain
of being ignored and useless
till one day when it's nowhere to be found
Wife said: it's been taken away by the recycling people
and I've paid five bucks for the cost of removal
which reminds me of someone
who has left no trace
in the world where he's spent his short life
nothing good worth remembering
and when he leaves
he needs people to see him off

喜宴

小B打来电话，要我去喝喜酒
结婚的喜酒，喜来登小酒店
县城很普通的一家，场面不大
莫不是他也换了女人
第二次结婚屡见不鲜
老实巴交的小B，做小工
贩古董，十几年含辛茹苦
刚刚砌了一栋两层小楼
灶间生火，祠堂冒烟
老婆贤惠漂亮，沉默寡言
多么可惜，这一段婚姻
多么可怜，他们的五个子女
（最小的是儿子）
婚礼那天，天气有点沉闷
我满怀好奇去看一次表演
——小B和他老婆笑脸相迎
呵呵，多么奇怪的婚礼
补婚？多么新鲜的词汇
补漏，补缺，补课，补酒

小B只是想补回一张脸面

——给老婆补一次红妆

Wedding Banquet

Little B called to ask me to attend his wedding banquet

at Hilton, a small hotel

an ordinary one in the county city, not a grand occasion

has he replaced his woman?

second marriages these days are not infrequent

an ingenuous and hard-working sort, Little B has worked as a labourer

a dealer in antiques and has been working hard for more than a decade

he's just built a two-storey house

a fire in the hearth and smoke in the chimney

his wife kind-hearted and pretty, short of words

what a pity this marriage is

how miserable their five kids are

(the youngest a son)

on the day of the wedding ceremony, the weather was dismal

full of curiosity, I went to see the performance

—Little B and his wife met me with smiling faces

well, what a strange wedding

did they say 'a makeup marriage'? What a new term

stopping a hole, filling up a vacancy, makeup classes and adding more cups all Little B ever wanted to do is to make up for his lost face

—to make his wife up in red

末日之诗

我们把这一天当作最后一天
平常不敢说的话都说出来
过去不敢做的事大胆去做
呵，真好！世界末日
我要好好爱你，爱你一天，一个晚上
还要第二天黎明的一个小时
我要把所有的甜言蜜语说够
我要把所有的活做完，重活累活
快活慢活，一口气做完，做完
就放下自己，就万事大吉

Poem of the Doomsday

we all treat the day as the doomsday

on which we say the unsayable

and do the undoable

oh, it's so good! Doomsday

I'll love you well, for a day, and for a night

and for one hour the next dawn

I'll say all the sweet nothings till I run out of them

I'll finish doing all the work, all the heavy and tiring work

all the quick and slow work, in one breath, till I finish it all

when I'll lay myself down before it's done

下棋

常常自己跟自己下棋
一会儿执黑，一会儿执白
把自己作为对手
是否会轻松一些？

不必咬牙切齿
不必你死我活
无非要论个胜负
无非是我和另一个我抗争

落地生根，下子无悔
我们打个平手如何？
我答应，另一个我不罢休
于是。死棋。

呵呵，自己跟自己下棋
知根知底，不用心计
有时觉得无所谓
有时真的纠结

Playing Go

I often play go with myself
taking the black or the white
would treating myself as an opponent
make it easier?

one wouldn't have to gnaw one's teeth
or to engage in a life-or-death struggle
just to win the game
for, after all, I am fighting against another I

when a move is made, I don't retract it
how about we achieve a tie?
I agree, but another I doesn't
hence a dead piece

ah, well, when I play go with myself
I know it through and through and I'm not calculating
sometimes I don't care
but, at other times, I really do

小胖

小胖上面有两个姐姐，没有爸爸妈妈
爸爸到很远很远的地方打工去了，几年没有回家
妈妈也出去打工了，后来跟别的男人走了
小胖是七十多岁的奶奶一手带大的
一个喝凉水都能长大的孩子
小胖这根独苗长得又粗又壮
但有点歪，像一棵歪脖子树
树干结多，根系卧在乱石底下
我问他成绩好不好，他说不好
我问他喜不喜欢读书，他说不喜欢
我问他的理想是什么，他说不知道
我问他喜欢做什么，他说打游戏
我问他想不想爸爸妈妈，他说不想
我问他会做什么有什么特长
他说回家会跟奶奶挑水
他力气大，扳手腕全班第一
他还给我背了一首古诗，两个
错别字让他一阵脸红，我知道
他使出了吃奶的力气——

小胖沐浴着春天的阳光
他的土壤缺少些许养料

Little Fat

Little Fat has two older sisters but no mum or dad near him
his dad working far, far away from home, not home for years
and his mum, too, who then left with another man
Little Fat was brought up by his grandma, aged 70
a boy who could have grown up on mere cold water
Little Fat, this sole seedling, is thick and strong
a little crooked, like a crooked-neck tree
with many knots on the trunk, its roots lying under the riprap of stones
when I asked how he did at school, he said not good
when I asked if he liked reading, he said no
when I asked what his ideal was, he said he didn't know
when I asked what he liked, he said he liked playing video games
when I asked if he missed his parents, he said no
when I asked what he was good at
he said he could carry water for Grandma, with a shoulder pole
and he said he had strength as he was best at wrist wrestling
he recited a classical poem for me but blushed at the two mistakes
he had made. I knew
that he had used up all his strength—

Little Fat was bathing in the sunlight of the spring
although his soil lacked nutrition

反刍

刚吃完饭——
米饭的味道
青菜的味道
辣椒的味道
普洱茶的味道
杂揉在嘴角的右边
未曾反刍的胃里
突然冒出你身体的味道
它们汇合在一起，五味杂陈
记忆，在瞬间打开了一道闸门
仔细闻闻，那就是生活的味道
一个孤独的男人的味道……

Ruminating

just had dinner—
the taste of the rice
of the vegetables
of the chili
and of the Pu'er tea
all mixed to the right corner of my mouth
suddenly, the taste of your own body
surged from within the stomach that had never ruminated
to merge together, with five different tastes
memory, in that instant, opened its sluicegate
on closer smelling, it was the taste of life
that of a solitary man's...

科隆大教堂

我所见到的科隆大教堂
有三种颜色：金色，金黄色，铁灰色
这是太阳在不同时间段
给它镀上去的
有500年前的
也有100年前的
还有今天傍晚的
从底座到高高尖顶
神在上面，人在下面

The Cologne Cathedral

the Cologne Cathedral I've seen
has three colours: golden, golden-yellow and iron grey
colours that the sun has coated it with
in different periods of time
one colour 500 years ago
another 100 years ago
and still another this evening
from the base to the tall spire
God above and man below

一张纸

一张纸可以写最美的文字
一张纸可以决定一个人的命运
当纸和铅字结合在一起
背后肯定有一台操纵的机器
以及一批操纵机器的人
这些人躲在幕后
将一张纸涂涂改改
将一台机器弄得脏兮兮
一张纸其实没有什么
了不起，放在我的手里
只能写一些无用的诗句

A Piece of Paper

one could draw the best pictures on a piece of paper

and the fate of an individual could be determined by a piece of paper

when a piece of paper is combined with a type

there must be a manipulating machine behind it

along with a group of people manipulating it

who are hiding behind the scene

tampering with what's on the paper

making a mess of the machine

a piece of paper really is

nothing, as it, lying in my hand

enables me to write a few useless lines only

玫瑰，其实只是一种花

红红的，天鹅绒般的红玫瑰
白白的，白云彩似的白玫瑰
它们是一种花的颜色
或者说，是一种布的背景
那一朵紫色的玫瑰
就像姐姐出嫁时的内衣

玫瑰花在不同的季节绽放
在它们悠悠长长的沁香里
有一种情结让人怀想
有一种比喻不需要解释
为什么诗人总把玫瑰比作爱情
这就是一朵花，从乡村到城里的象征

玫瑰，其实只是一种花
我必须经常为她培土、整枝和浇水

Roses, Really, are a Variety of Flowers

a red, red rose, like velvet
a white, white rose, like a cloud
they are the colour of a flower
or the background of a cloth
the purple rose
resembles the underclothes Older Sister wore at the wedding

roses open in various seasons
there's a lingering fragrance in them
and a complex that needs no explanation
why do poets compare a rose to love
whereas it's a mere flower, the symbol both for the country and for the city

roses, really, are a variety of flowers
that I have to keep watering, cultivating and pruning

对岸油菜花开

一点点。一簇簇。一片片。
在夕阳的余晖里，金黄的油菜花
由远而近。一群蜜蜂用细长的手臂
将晚风轻轻摇动。用利齿
将阳光轻轻咬碎。酿一缕清香、一丝甜蜜
此刻风景宜人
站在河堤看对岸油菜花开
我的目光由远而近

The Canola Flowers on the Other Side of the River

Dots. Clusters. Spreads.

in the afterglow, the golden canola flowers

come from afar. A group of bees, with their slender arms

are gently shaking the evening wind and, with their sharp teeth

are biting the sun into pieces, brewing fragrances and sweetness

the scene, at this moment, is gorgeous

standing on the bank, watching the canola flowers in bloom across the river

I watch, my eye getting close

金黄的稻子

农民挥镰之前，久久地缄默
久久地注目，弯腰鞠躬
金黄的稻子在秋风里不语
河水静静流淌，循环往复
如果可能，我想把时光挽留
把一束稻子的小小幸福，捧在手中

Golden Ears of Rice

Before the peasants swing their sickles, they fall into a long silence
and they watch for a long time, making a bow with their bent backs
Golden ears of rice are wordless in the autumn wind
The river flows quietly, repetitiously
If I could, I would retain time
and hold the small happiness of an ear of rice, in my hand

倒影

一只飞鸟的影子
飘在河面，它让我看到了
三种独立的风景
一座桥通往城里
它的流动步履匆匆
一棵树长在水边
它的向往生动、纯净
一座古塔在岸边祈祷
它的坚持就是沉默

Reflections

the reflection of a bird

was drifting across the river so that I saw

three independent scenes:

a bridge to the city

with a flow of hurried footsteps

a tree growing by the waterside

its aspirations vivid and pure

and an ancient pagoda, praying by the riverbank

with silence its persistence

钟点工彩云儿

钟点工彩云儿在58岁这一年

终于把她的男人赶走了

这一年她的男人才43岁

身强力壮，还可以结婚生子

他们相爱了整整23年

从这个城市的街头爱到街尾

从出租屋的夜晚爱到白天

他们相爱的时候，彩云儿35岁

离过一次婚，有三个孩子

而爱她的男人才刚刚20，无拘无束

只因为那一个夜晚他多看了她一眼

只因为她说了一句：我是一朵流浪的云

两朵无家可归的云碰在一起

下了一场酣畅淋漓的雨

这一个雨季抚河潮起潮涌

这一个秋天金黄的稻穗一望无际

日子在无声无息中交替

爱，在锅碗瓢盆中延伸

她一边擦洗玻璃，一边回忆爱情

幸福的时光在一片湿布上漫延

Cai Yun'er, a Part-Time Maid

Cai Yun'er, a part-time maid, managed to chase her man out

when she was 58

and her man was 43

a man still strong enough to remarry with kids

they'd been in love for 23 years

from the head of the street to the end of it in this city

and from nights in a rented room to days

when they fell in love, Cai Yun'er was 35

having divorced, with three kids

and her man was just past 20, free on his own

it's not till he took an extra look at her that night

and she said: I'm a vagrant cloud

that the two homeless clouds collided

and merged into a full rain

in this rainy season, the Fuhe River surged with a rushing tide

and in this autumn, the golden ears of rice stretched as far as the eye could

     see

days alternated in total silence

and love, extending amongst the pots and pans

as she was cleaning the glasses and recalled her love

the happy time was spreading over a piece of wet cloth

一块石头的硬和冷

我手握一块坚硬的石头
它体内的热早已被大自然吸干
一身怀远、思乡的病
冰凉，偏执，一硬到底
你无法触摸它的内心
它来自水流湍急的山溪
有天然质朴和野性的美
傲然，决绝，一意孤行
你不能触及它的灵魂
我把它放置于书桌
目光不敢停留太久
硬和冷，寒彻心骨
也许它是一块璞玉
也许它是天外之物
作为艺术或摆设
它一点也不神奇
我不停地摩擦
先是微凉，再是微热
然后满脸潮红
濡湿了我的手心

The Hardness and Coldness of a Stone

I'm holding a hard stone
its inner heat long dried up by nature
a stone sick with nostalgia and a longing for the faraway
icy-cold and stubborn, hard to the core
you can't touch the heart of its hearts
it came from a mountain creek of rapid flows
and it carries a natural simplicity and wild beauty
proud and resolute, a law onto itself
you can't touch its soul
when I placed it on the desk
my eye dared not linger over it
so hard and cold my heart-bone was chilled
perhaps it's an unpolished gem
or something that came from beyond the skies
not magical at all
as art or decoration
I kept rubbing it
when it turned from cool to a faint heat
till its face was flushed
wetting the heart of my hand

诗，酒，李白和油菜花

不会喝酒，还能写诗
他们中许多人提出质疑
并说李白，斗酒诗百篇
而你滴酒不沾，似乎还讨厌
似乎以酒为敌。你不作解释
继续拒酒千里之外，继续
写诗，发表在老家的菜地和
现在居住的小镇的青石板上
它长出绿色的叶子和结痂的
青苔，这些都与生活有关
它长出五谷杂粮的粗砺
和灰暗日子的湿滑，这些
与李白无关，与酒无关
在这可爱的季节，他也会
抒情，比如面对春天的油菜花
扑面而来的清香，和可以预见

的饱满的菜籽，他写下了：
春风里的油菜花心旌摇荡
它像一个醉酒的诗人，在
浪漫主义和现实主义的意境里
它一点不像李白，而更像杜甫

Poetry, Drinking, Li Bai and the Canola Flowers

if you don't drink, how can you possibly write poetry?

that's a question many of them ask and they say

if Li Bai could write hundreds of poems when engaging in a battle of
  spirits

how can you if you never touch a drop, detest it

and regard it as an enemy? You, though, don't explain

and you continue to keep the spirits at arm's length and keep writing

poetry, publishing them in the vegetable plots of your old home

and on the bluestones in the small town where you live

so that they grow green leaves and scabbed

moss, all relevant to living

and they grow the grittiness of five cereals

and the slippage of dark days, all

irrelevant to Li Bai or to liquor

in this lovely season, he, too, will become

lyrical. For example, when faced with the spring canola flowers

and the fragrance rushing in his face, and with the predicted

full seeds, he wrote:

the canola flowers are waving their heart banners in the spring wind like a drunken poet, in the state-of-mind *yijing* of romanticism and realism resembling Du Fu much more than Li Bai

一列春天的火车从梨园开出

谁想阻止春天的脚步

谁就是个犯罪的人

预谋不让某一笺梨花落地

某一个花蕊结果

那都是徒劳

我在想，这个春天属于每一个人

为什么有人悲伤，有人欢喜

有人迈不开脚步

有人在恣意奔跑

呵，梨花开满山凹——

一列春天的火车从梨园开出

一个春天的妄想随梨花飞扬

我要说，留住春天的方式

不是别人举起的相机

是你张开的双臂和笑脸

是一朵梨花盛开过几次

A Spring Train Coming out of the Pear Garden

whoever wants to stop the spring in its tracks

must be a criminal

it would be a vain attempt

to plot against a pear flower from falling

or a stamen from coming to fruition

but I'm thinking to myself that this spring belongs to everyone

why, I mean, some are sad and some are happy

some can't step out

while others are running without restraint

oh, the pear flowers are filling the hollow of a hill—

a spring train is coming out of the pear garden

and a spring fantasy is set aloft with the pear flowers

all I want to say is that the only way to retain the spring

is not the cameras held up by others

but your open arms and smiling face

a pear flower, blooming more than once

石榴

一面潮湿的灰墙上
一颗石榴寂然裂开
在这暧昧的午后
不要对她的情欲说三道四
不要对她的液汁垂涎欲滴
更不要虚幻的赞美和说词
任由一缕细碎的秋风把岁月吹薄
任由一丝微凉的秋雨把内衣濡湿
并等她静静地和月亮一起坠
                落
              坠
            落

The Pomegranate

on a wet grey wall

a pomegranate cracked open, in its solitariness

in this ambiguous afternoon

stop carping about its lust

stop mouth-watering for its oozing liquid

and stop the vain praising words

but just let the broken autumnal breeze thin the years

and let the cool autumnal rain moisten the underclothes

while waiting for her to quietly fall with the

                    m

                    o

                    o

                    n

肚脐眼，第三只眼

她就是不睁开
任你抚摸，任你亲吻
任你急切地进入她的腹地
她就是不听
她说，她怕羞
怕看见你离她那么近
那么深邃的海洋
会把她淹没
于是，她闭上所有的眼睛
任湖水荡漾，鱼儿嬉戏
她看见火焰，在身体内部
以水的方式燃烧
以雾的方式缠绕

The Belly Button, a Third Eye

refusing to open

she lets you touch and kiss

and she lets you enter, in a hurry, into her bellyland

she refuses to listen

and she says: she is shy

and she is afraid of you so close to her

for such a deep sea

might drown her

so she closes all her eyes

to let the lake water undulate and the fish play

she watches the flames burning inside the body

the way water moves

and getting entangled, the way fog does

赞美

——致杜拉斯

当茉莉花在十二月的黄昏
飘来淡淡的清香
我突然想起了你，杜拉斯
你的一生是一部后现代
小说：爱，爱情和性
没有谋篇布局，和矫情
只有人性的光辉，和诗意的美
文字中流着法兰西的血液
塞纳河的安静和涌动
情到深处，水流无声
如果与你在湄公河上的相遇
我也会爱上你，和你的皱纹
爱上你，黄昏中的倒影
亲爱的，杜拉斯……

Praise

To Duras

the jasmine flowers were carrying their faint fragrances
through the December dusk
when I thought of you, Duras
your life a postmodern
fiction: love, emotion and sex
no plotting or scheming, no pretensions
only things lit up with humanity and a beauty of poetry
french blood running through your words
in a Seine of surging quietness
when emotion reaches the depths, waters run silent
I'd fall in love with you, and with your wrinkles
if we met on the Mekong
and I'd fall in love with your reflection at dusk
dear Duras...

中华小学

先在一个庙里
后在一个祠堂
我小学毕业廿年后
它搬迁至一个山岗
四间砖瓦房是教室
也是老师宿舍、办公的地方
食堂和厕所挨得很近很紧
操场上几只雀鸟叽叽喳喳
一条跛脚的跑道
半是砂石，半是泥土
——中华，中华小学
念叨这个响亮的名字
看见迎风飘扬的国旗
我想起伟大的天安门
和天安门上的毛主席

A Chinese Primary School

first it's located in a temple
then in a clan hall
20 years after I graduated from it
it's shifted to the top of a hill
four tiled brick houses serving as its classrooms
staff quarters and offices
the canteen close to the toilet
birds chirping on the sports ground
a lame track
half gravel and half mud
—Chinese, a Chinese primary school
murmuring the resounding name
and watching the National Flag flying
I recalled the Great Tiananmen
and Chairman Mao on it

一块抹布

从一块新布
到一块旧布
再到一块抹布

身上的色彩
越来越少
体内的毒素
越来越多

这是一个人的蜕变
也是一个人的一生

"这一生很短啊，
怎么活成这等模样！"

A Mop

from a new cloth
to an old one
then to a mop

its colour reduced
to less and less
as it gathered more and more
poison

the metamorphosis of a person
and the life of one, too

'how can a life, so short
have been lived to such a shape?'

父与子

错
错错
错错错
错错错错
错错错错错
错错错错错错

没有一个对
统统都是错！
知道错了吗？
错在哪儿啦？
知错能改么？
错了还会错吗？

父亲咬牙切齿
儿子嗫嚅着说——
都是你和我妈的错！

Father and Son

wrong

wrong, wrong

wrong, wrong, wrong

wrong, wrong, wrong, wrong

wrong, wrong, wrong, wrong, wrong

wrong, wrong, wrong, wrong, wrong, wrong

nothing right

all wrongs!

know you are in the wrong?

but where is it wrong?

if you know, can you right the wrong?

already wrong, how can it be righted?

the father is gnawing his teeth

and the son, haltingly, said—

but you and Mom are to blame, for your wrong!

烧纸

在小区的一块空地
有人点香，烧纸
放起噼噼啪啪的爆竹

哦，清明又到了！

坟，早就迁走了
但祖宗的遗训还在，阴魂还在

或许，怨气还在……

Burning the Paper

on an empty lot in the small residential district
someone has lit up the incense and burns the paper money
setting off the firecrackers

ah, well, it's the Qingming Festival again!

the grave has long gone
but the ancestral teachings of the deceased linger, along with their ghosts

and, perhaps, their resentment still remains...

同学老丁

一件西装穿了近十年
皮鞋补了三次还在穿
在同学里面，他是富翁
有三个店面
不抽烟，不打牌
偶尔跟我们去钓鱼
老婆给的零用钱
攒到一起
一个月两次
去找女人
我们说到这些
他只嘿嘿一笑——
"谁不爱年轻的肉体……"

Old Ding, My Classmate

the suit on him has been worn for nearly a decade
and his leather shoes, repaired three times, are still there with his feet
he's rich, among my old classmates
he runs three shops
he doesn't smoke or play cards
occasionally, he goes fishing, with us
he puts together the pocket money
his wife gives him
and pays the women
he seeks out twice a month
when we talk about this
he laughs and says—
'but who doesn't love the young flesh...?'

力量和见证

这宁静的湖面
有好大的鱼
许多人不相信
钓鱼的人也不信
但我刚刚看到
它掀起的浪花
波及大半个湖面

Power and Witness

the lake is placid

there are big fish

but many don't believe it

even the fishermen don't

still, the wave it churned up

that I've just seen

spreads across more than half of the lake's length

孤独的孩子

欧阳昱先生
把我的一首诗
翻译成英文
发表在澳洲
的一本杂志上

就像一个孩子
在一个陌生的国度　　流浪
就像太平洋的一朵浪花
在澳洲昆士兰海滩徘徊

The Solitary Child

Mr Ouyang Yu
has turned one of my poems
into English
and published it in an Australian
magazine

like a child
wandering   in a strange country
like the flower of a wave in the Pacific
pacing, to and fro, on a Queensland beach

哭坟

一丘不大的黄土堆

一个头发篷乱的女人

一场孤零零的诉说和呼喊

一阵黎明时就下个不停的苦雨

哭声由远而近，一阵紧似一阵

她呼天抢地哭喊儿子的名字

她声音凄凉数落儿子的不是

她咒丈夫不把她当人

她怨自己没护好唯一的根苗

她揪打自己伤心的过去

她泣说自己命苦

她哭累了

就趴在儿子身上

陷在那片薄土里

再也没有力气爬起来

Crying over the Tomb

a small mound of yellow earth
a woman with straggly hair
a solitary pouring of grief and crying
a bitter rain that has been going on since dawn
the crying is now moving closer, becoming more urgent
lamenting to the sky, uttering the name of her son
in a bleak voice, she blamed her son for everything
and she condemned her husband for treating her inhumanly
she blamed herself for not safeguarding her only seedling
she beat up her heart-broken past
and she, in tears, said that she had had a hard lot
when she tired herself out crying
she groveled over her son
sinking into that thin layer of earth
no longer able to pick herself up

6和9

正看是6

反看是9

像一对情侣

做一种游戏

它有音乐的旋律

也有工笔的简洁

动感十足的画面

力和美的完美体现

它是吉祥的象征

世俗生活的延伸

从6到9，爬两座山

从9到6，下三层楼

两个圆圈和两根手指

暗中较劲，颠来倒去

一个向上，一个向下

一个向右，一个向左

有眼睛翻来覆去的旋涡

有不知身在何处的幻影

从6到9，从9到6

时间，它走了相反的方向

快慢互肘，慢是快的节奏
在一个点上，它停了下来
一个乾，一个坤
一个阳，一个阴
天地人同道
6和9合一

6 and 9

6 if looked at this way

9, that way

like a couple

engaging in a game

with musical rhythms

and simplicity of brushwork

a dynamic picture

and a perfect epitome of power and beauty

a symbol of auspiciousness

an extension of secular life

from 6 to 9, climbing two mountains

from 9 to 6, down three storeys

two circles and two fingers

in secret rivalry, turning upside down

one going up, the other coming down

one turning right, the other, left

with a whirlpool of tossing eyes

and with apparitions of bodylessness

from 6 to 9 and from 9 to 6

time has now travelled to the opposite direction

fastness and slowness cross-elbowed, slowness being the rhythm of fastness

till it stops at one spot

one being Qian and the other, Kun

both part of the Eight Diagrams

one being Yang and the other, Yin

the heaven, the earth and the wo/man in the same track

6 and 9 merging into one

爱情是一只爬虫

爱情是一只爬虫

爬来爬去，一刻不停

先爬到手心

然后爬到手臂

然后爬上他的心

然后爬到她的脚底

爬过鲜嫩的肉体和灵魂

爬过一个饭团和苹果的尸体

痒，在红点上

痛，在疤痕内

她捧着一颗星星

对他说：好美！

Love is a Crawling Insect

love is a crawling insect

constantly crawling

first onto the heart of the hand

up the arm

reaching his heart

then down to the bottom of her foot

across the tender flesh and soul

and past a ball of rice and the corpse of an apple

the red spot getting itchy

and the scar, painful

she, holding a star in both hands

said to him: so beautiful!

失眠的小虫

"吱吱，吱吱吱"
"吱吱，吱吱吱"
……，……
这是午夜两点
最绝望的声音……

The Insomniac Insect

'squeak, squeak, squeak'

'squeak, squeak, squeak'

… , … ,

the sound in absolute despair

at 2 a.m.

月光下，金黄的稻穗

一把银色的镰刀
在头上晃来晃去
恐惧，骚乱，暴动
瞬间掀起的革命
始于一阵风的兴起
和消弭。夜，越来越深
一头雾水的头颅
在等待不可知的命运

Under the Moonlight, the Golden Ears of Rice

a silver sickle

was moving above my head

with fear, disturbance and riot

as a revolution, kicked up in an instant

began with the rise and fall

of a wind. Night, deepening

the head, wrapped up in a fog

was waiting for the unknown fate

旧鞋

这是一双旧鞋
别人穿过，现在你穿
木心说，旧的空鞋都有脚
一些重重叠叠的脚印
湿淋淋，从鞋缝里跑了出来
脚印与脚印，有的臭味相投
有的互相诋毁，像情敌
脚的影子跟鬼一样
被你狠狠地踩在底下
又死死地附在你的心上

A Pair of Old Shoes

this is a pair of old shoes
that someone else has worn and that you are now wearing
according to Wooden Heart (Mu Xin), empty old shoes have feet
footsteps, overlapped and wet
have come running out of their seams
footsteps, sharing the same rotten smells
or running each other down, like rivals in love
the shadow of the feet, like ghosts
are trodden by you underneath
but that are attached, like death, to your heart

钉子打进去之后

一位老人
往树上打钉子
他打一下我痛一下
就像打进我的肉体
一阵紧似一阵
一直打到第五下
我就失去了感觉
三十多年过去
老人早已作古
树长得又高又大
可是，我的心
为什么——
还在隐隐作痛

When the Nail was Hammered In

an old man

was hammering a nail into a tree

each hit pained me

as if he was nailing it in my flesh

one hit following another

closely, more closely

till, when he hit the fifth hit

I lost my consciousness

thirty years on

the old man is long gone

why—

is my heart

still in pain?

下棋

他们是退休的老人
进城的务工人员，以及
附近小商店的经营者
每天下午五点钟左右
他们把棋盘摆在街边
一对一地厮杀、较量
令周围的空气严肃紧张
——博弈者凝神敛气
围观者心急如焚，一时间
楚河汉界，风起云涌
气氛随棋子而波动
输，或者赢，是必然的结局
偶然中的一盘和棋，会让
其中的一些人愤愤不平
另一些人耿耿于怀

Playing Chess

these are the old retirees

workers in the city, originally from the country, and

the nearby shop-owners

around 5pm each day

they lay the chessboard by the roadside

one battling against the other, in rivalry

the air intense around them

—the chess-fighters holding their breath

the onlookers, torn with anxiety. Instantly

a storm is raised on either side of the board

the atmosphere fluctuating with each move

the inevitable endgame is, inevitably, a win or a loss

an occasional draw will cause

some of them to get angry

and others, to brood on the injury

熟人

在这个再熟悉不过的城市
每天都会遇到几个再熟悉不过的人
米粉摊上，上班路上，公交车上
点头，问好，说说天气
在超市，在饭馆，在茶楼
对视，闲聊，儿女情长
由不熟悉到熟悉
是偶然，也是必然
它拉近了人与人的距离
它让生活在挤匝中慢慢淡去
我怕见人，怕见人无话可说
不愿点头哈腰，不愿
无话找话，更不愿无事八卦
朋友从广东带来年轻女友
他说要去处理公务，要我
带她去走走，转转，看看
朋友的信任让我惴惴不安
一个年轻漂亮陌生的女子
莺莺燕燕走在我的身边
那是你朋友么？人家没问

我就不知如何是好，就紧张
——哦，她是我朋友的朋友
在心里我一遍又一遍地念叨

Acquaintances

in this city more familiar than familiar itself

I daily encounter a number of people more familiar than familiar itself

at the rice noodle stand, on my way to work or on board a bus

I nod, I greet them, and I talk about the weather

in a supermarket, a restaurant or a teahouse

we look at each other, we chat, and we indulge in nonsense

growing from unfamiliar to familiar

an accidental but inevitable process

that shortens the distance between people

and that thins life in the squeeze of the crowd

although I, for one, am afraid of meeting people, of having nothing much
    to say

as I don't like to nod and bow nor do I

like trying to make small talk, least of talking behind someone's back

when a friend brought his younger girlfriend from Guangdong

and said that he was going somewhere else to do business, leaving her

to me, for me to show her around

the place, this trust made me nervous

with a young, pretty woman

like an oriole by my side

is this your friend? Without people asking

I already lost my nerve

—ah, well, she's my friend's friend
I kept saying that to myself, at heart

不快乐的一天

这一天的不快乐一个接着一个

早上被吵醒没睡够不快乐

早餐吃了两个鸡蛋一碗米粉味精太多不快乐

交通拥堵上班迟到半小时不快乐

物价还在上涨股票还在下跌不快乐

天气闷热思维迟钝不快乐

许多事情想做不知如何去做不快乐

无所事事一个半小时不快乐

突然停电半小时不快乐

接到儿子莫名其妙的电话不快乐

（他爱的女孩人家不爱他不快乐）

不知道如何去爱不快乐

不知道如何安慰儿子不快乐

过生日父母都不在不快乐

请人喝酒喝到假酒不快乐

又长了两斤赘肉不快乐

农历七月十五发出一条短信收到四条短信不快乐

晚上看到橙色满月高挂在不明亮的夜空不快乐

看电视广告太多爱情剧太滥不快乐

中国人登上自己的钓鱼岛被扣押不快乐

跟人交流不快乐

一个人独处不快乐

我不快乐你更不快乐

女儿考上大学不快乐

上大学要去很远的地方不快乐

去很远的地方上大学需要很多钱不快乐

一个父亲拿不出很多钱给女儿上大学不快乐

想改变现状又无可奈何不快乐

三更半夜胡思乱想对自己咬牙切齿不快乐

看书看到罗素说两个不快乐的原因还是不快乐

有钱不快乐没钱更不快乐

内心不快乐表面装不出快乐

你不快乐写在脸上刻在身上

我不快乐写在纸上刻在流水的弧线上

An Unhappy Day

things unhappy that day followed one after another

I wasn't happy because I hadn't slept enough when woken up in the
  morning

I wasn't happy because there was too much MSG in my rice noodle with
  two eggs

I wasn't happy because I was half an hour late, held up in the traffic

I wasn't happy because the price was going up and the stocks were falling

I wasn't happy because the weather was too hot, dulling my mind

I wasn't happy because there were too many things I didn't know how to do

I wasn't happy because I had nothing much to do for one hour and a half

I wasn't happy because there was a power cut for half an hour

I wasn't happy because I got a strange call from my son

(the girl he loved didn't love him back)

I wasn't happy because I didn't know how to love

I wasn't happy because I didn't know how to comfort my son

I wasn't happy because my parents were not at my birthday party

I wasn't happy because I drank fake liquor when inviting people to dinner

I wasn't happy because I had gained one kilo of proud flesh

I wasn't happy because I got only 4 texts in return for my text on July 15

I wasn't happy because I saw an orange full moon on a sky none too bright

I wasn't happy because there were too many sentimental TV dramas on TV

I wasn't happy because Chinese were detained when they landed in their
  own Senkaku Islands

I wasn't happy communicating with people

I wasn't happy being alone

I wasn't happy with you being more unhappy

I wasn't happy because my daughter succeeded in passing the exam for a
    university

I wasn't happy because the university was far away from home

I wasn't happy because that would involve me having to pay heaps of
    money

I wasn't happy being unable to change the status quo despite my thoughts

I wasn't happy thinking wild thoughts at midnight and gnawing my teeth

I wasn't happy even when I learnt about Russell's two causes of
    unhappiness

I wasn't happy either with money or without money

I wasn't able to pretend to be happy when I didn't feel happy at heart

when you aren't happy you have it written on your face and your body

when I'm unhappy I write it down and carve it on the curves of running
    waters

十年一觉

有人买了房

有人买了车

有人上了大学

有人去了国外

有人结婚生子

有人做了爷爷奶奶

有人连升三级

有人成了穷光蛋

有人长了几斤肉

有人去了另一个世界

有人谈了N次恋爱

有人长了几根白发

有人傍了大款

有人失去天下

有人得了神经病

有人跳楼自杀

有人出过几本书

有人不说一句人话

有人看过一次电影

有人天天洗桑拿

有人做过一件好事

有人进过几次监狱

有人写了一首口语诗

有人在她面前流口水

有人到月球上走了一圈

有人到地狱滚了几回

有人丢了一根肋骨

有人多了半边后脑勺

有人去过非洲

有人去过马来西亚

有人进城打工没有回过一次家

有人上访，在归来的路上

有人睡了一觉

有人还没有醒来

A Decade Long Sleep

some have bought houses

some have bought cars

some have gone to university

some have gone abroad

some have got married with kids

some have become granddads and grandmas

some have advanced through the ranks by three levels

some have become poor bastards

some have gained a few kilos

some have gone to another world

some have fallen in and out of love for the nth time

some have grown a few grey hairs

some have secured themselves sugar daddies

some have lost their underheavens

some have fallen mentally ill

some have jumped to their death

some have published a few books

some have never said anything human

some have only been to the movies once

some have daily sauna

some have done only one good thing

some have gone to jail a number of times

some have written an oral poem

some have mouth-watered in front of her

some have gone around the moon

some have rolled a number of times in hell

some have lost a rib

some have lost half of their brains at the back

some have been to Africa

some have been to Malaysia

some have never come home after they went working in the city

some have petitioned, now on their way home

some have slept

some have never woken up

一念

有人说我前世是出家人
我真的就相信了
前世，或者前前世
做了很多善事
度了很多人——
阿弥陀佛，功德圆满！
好不容易投胎到今生
可不可以做点"坏"事
这念头突然冒出
让我内心一惊
继而淡然一笑
——不杀人，也不抢劫
只是想补偿前世的亏欠
打牌，喝酒，近女色
不读诗经，不念心经
不那么一本正经……

A Thought

someone told me that I was a Buddhist monk

and I believe that I am

having done much good

in my previous life, my previous previous life

for many people—

Amitabha, rounding it all off

it wasn't easy that I have been reincarnated

can I do something 'bad'?

as soon as the thought visited me

I was taken aback

but I laughed

—killing no one nor robbing any

doing so only to make up for the losses of my previous life

playing cards, drinking and having sex

not reading *The Book of Songs* or *The Book of Heart*

not being so bloody serious...

一个物质主义者的抒情方式

比如说——

吃饭时发出吧嗒吧嗒的响声

睡觉时发出呼噜呼噜的鼾声

亲热时发出吭哧吭哧的叫声

物质主义者喜欢动词

拒绝形容词，他认为

抒情，应该来自身体本身

来自一个巨大的胃

和一个超级的肺

来自外界对肉体的刺激

而诗，就是垃圾

没有声音的垃圾

让人无法忍受

A Materialist's Lyrical Ways

for example—

making smacking sounds when eating

snoring when sleeping

making noisy sex when making love

a materialist loves verbs

and he refuses adjectives for he thinks

lyricism ought to come from body itself

from a huge stomach

superlative lungs

and the stimulation to the body from the outside world

meanwhile, poetry is rubbish

so soundless

one can hardly stand it

四十那年

那一天你轻轻地吻了我
我是在梦中　似醒非醒
感觉就像四十年前母亲的目光
轻轻洒落在我稚嫩的脸上

日子每天都这样过
上班。下班。有时跟女儿开开玩笑
偶尔也在书房呆上一天
散步时会跟你讲些书中的故事
而你似乎也编好了固定的程序
上课。下课。还有忙不完的家务活
买菜。做饭。洗衣。拖地……
饭桌上你会讲一些学生的事
咸咸淡淡也放些味精
印象最深的一次，你告诉我
一个学生家长，年龄和我们相仿
因为"网恋"而抛弃家庭
你的学生成了断线的风筝
万里无云的天空飘着你的忧虑

那一刻，你的表情
正在演绎一幕电视剧
你愤怒的眼神唏嘘不已
（你羡慕我们的邻居
一对退休的老人，他们从不上网
偶尔会在麻将桌上消磨时光）

那一天你轻轻地吻了我
我已经梦醒 并且激动不已
感觉就像四十年后你长满皱纹的双手
轻轻抚摸我满头的白发

In the Year When I Reached 40

that day you gave me a gentle kiss
I was in a dream   half-awake
feeling as if my mother's eyes, forty years before
had fallen on my infantile face

each day went, just like that
going to, and from, work. I'd sometimes crack jokes with my
daughter
and, occasionally, stay in my study for a whole day
when going out for a walk, I'd tell you of the stories I had read
and you seemed to have set some fixed programs
in and out of classes. Doing laundry. Mopping the floor...
you'd talk about your students over the dinner table
seasoning it with some MSG
I was most impressed when you revealed
that a student's parent, about our age
had abandoned his family as a result of 'internet love'
leaving your student like a kite on a broken line
your worries set adrift in a cloudless sky

in that instant, you acted as if
you were playing in a TV drama

marveling at it, with angry looks

(you admired our neighbours

a couple living in their retirement who never went online

and, occasionally, they would while away their time at the

mahjongg table)

that day, you gave me a gentle kiss

but I had woken up, and was quite excited

feeling as if your wrinkled hands, forty years after

were gently touching my head, full of grey hair

归途

我来到这个陌生的地方
就像当初来到
这个陌生的世界
我两手空空而来
就像当年赤身裸体而来
熙来攘往的旅程
我唯一的行李
是我的身体
坐动车，或乘飞机
都不需要托运
偶尔需要寄存的物件
是一颗疲惫的心

A Return Journey

when I arrived at this strange place

it was like my first arrival

in this strange world

I arrived empty-handed

like when I arrived naked

in the hustle and bustle of the journey

my only luggage

was my body

whether I travelled by train or plane

I had no need to check in

the only thing that is occasionally required to deposit

is a weary heart

绳子

我所有的噩梦

跟一根门杠有关

不是对不上眼

就是明显短了

对面有一个吊死鬼

她是我一切噩梦的根源

18岁跟堂哥结婚

19岁怀孕七个月

有一天夜里用一根绳子

结束了两条生命，第二天

早上我看到她模糊的面容

黑压压的人群里矮了半截的堂哥

长长的舌头和长长人群

她的婆婆不见了踪影

娘家人要捉他抵命……

我不到十岁的好奇和阴影

从此吊在一根门杠上

堂哥今年七十有二

一辈子单身无后

和半截影子度过

The Rope

all my nightmares

have to do with a wooden door bar

it either doesn't fit in

or is obviously too short

there is the ghost of a hanged woman on the opposite side

the source of all my nightmares

at 18, she married my cousin

at 19, seven months into her pregnancy

she, using a rope, ended two lives

on a night. The next

morning I saw her obscure features

my cousin who seemed to have shortened by half among the dark crowd

the long tongues and a long throng of people

her mother-in-law gone without a trace

her own family wanting to catch him, to pay her life with his own...

my curiosity as a 10-year-old and the shadow of all that

have since been hanging on the door bar

my cousin is 72 now

single all his life, without any children

a life that he has spent, with his half-shadow

我有西红柿一样的爱情

左手摸着空空的口袋
右手握着空空的锄头
播种，除草
施肥，捉虫子
这一切都在梦中进行
这山水田园长出的果实
我喜欢光溜溜的西红柿
西红柿炒蛋
是我的最爱
西红柿一样的爱情
酸里带甜，加上
小葱拌豆腐的美意
半截美梦里我
自己犒赏自己

I have a Love that is Like the Tomatoes

my left hand touching my empty pocket
my right hand holding an empty hoe
I am sowing the seeds, weeding the weeds
spreading the manure and catching the insects
all this is happening in a dream
of the fruit grown in this mountain-water garden
I like the naked tomatoes
and I love the tomatoes
fried with eggs best
love that is like the tomatoes
sour, with a little sweet, added
with a beautiful mind of chopped spring onion mixed with tofu
in the half remaining beautiful dream I
am now rewarding myself

诗

在你面前
我还是一个孩子
对世界的好奇
不仅止于文字
你的庙宇安放着
一颗俗世之心
奶汁抚平了皱纹
我拒绝长大
用一颗童心爱你

A Poem

facing you
I remain a child
my curiosity about the world
is not limited to the word
in your temple is placed
a vulgar heart
the wrinkles smoothed with milk
I love you with the heart of a child
refusing to grow up

野花开过了头

（和欧阳昱同题诗一首）

野花
疯了似地开
披头散发地开
不顾廉耻地开
赤身裸体地开
她真的疯了一样
在河滨公园

The Wild Flowers Overgrown

After Ouyang Yu, with a poem of the same title

the wild flowers

open like mad

disheveled

shameless

gone crazy

in the Riverside Park

窗前的树

开始画的
是幅草图
后来画的
是印象派
有点像莫奈
阳光也是淡淡的
接下来画的
是油画,浓浓的绿
滴了一地
最后
是一幅裸体
自己做模特
旁边
有一只黑鸟

The Tree in Front of the Window

it began

with a drawing

followed by

an impressionist one

a bit like Monet

the sunlight is also faint

what followed further

was an oil painting, thick with green

that was dripping, all over the floor

it all ended

with a nude

who was her own model

next to

a black bird

假专员之死

假文凭

假履历

假专员

假面具

假太师椅

假主席台

假鲜花

假掌声

假恭维

假马屁

什么都是假的

一纸判决书

和一颗子弹

是真的

Death of a Fake Commissioner

a fake diploma

a fake resume

a fake commissioner

a fake mask

a fake armchair, of the Imperial Tutor kind

a fake rostrum

fake fresh flowers

a fake applause

fake compliments

fake horse-fart flatteries

everything that is fake

except the written judgment

and a bullet

that are genuine

邻居小王

老公在广东打工
不是打仗
在几个城市打过
打得有些疲惫
有些泄气闷气
她带着三个儿女
从外县来到这个城市
安家，每天早上
送女儿上学
送儿子去幼儿园
再去菜市场
日子就这样重复
看不出她的年龄
她有什么样的工作
老公要赚钱
几个月回家一趟
有一天晚上11点到家
事先没有告知
三个孩子睡了
老婆不见踪影

第二天她脸上
有一道
闪电划下的痕迹

Little Wang, Our Neighbour

her hubby is working, not seeing action

in Guangdong

and has worked in a number of other cities

till he's quite weary

discouraged and depressed

she, with her three kids

has come to settle

in this city from

another county, where every morning

she would take her daughters to school

and her son to the kindergarten

before going to the vegetable market

days repeated thus

she didn't look her age

and what job she was doing

her hubby had to make money

and come home every few months

he did, on a night, at 11

without warning

the three kids asleep

and the wife nowhere to be seen

the next day, her face

was left with a trace

struck by a lightning

做旧

把房子做旧
修旧如旧
他的想法是
把自己也做旧
回到旧房子那年代
在慢生活的节奏里
喝一杯明清时的普洱
可生活无法回到从前
旧的总会有一些破绽
就像这把旧骨头
一不小心
就吱吱嘎嘎

Making It Old

making the house old
repairing it to look old
but his thought was
that he'd like to make himself old
till he returned to the year of old houses
and drank a cup of Pu'er, of the Ming and the Qing kind
in the rhythm of a slow life
but life refuses to return to the past
as the old always have flaws
like this handful of bones of mine
that creaks
on the off chance

买菜记

卖菜的阿婆
一个劲地说
自己的菜好
自家地里
种的空心菜
两块钱一斤
施农家肥
不打农药
她近乎
卑微的语气
和恳求的方式
让我对她的菜
和自己的判断
同时产生怀疑
接下来
的一个动作
更让我惊讶
用矿泉水瓶
来回往菜叶上洒水
好像她真的说了谎

要用一个谎言
掩盖更多的谎言

Buying the Vegetables

the granny selling the vegetables

kept saying

how good her vegetables were

the empty-hearted vegetable, or ong choi

that she had grown in her own vegetable plot

was priced at 4 yuan a kilo

and that had been enriched with the rural family manure

with no pesticide

her humble

way of talking

and entreating

led to my doubting

her vegetables

and my own judgment

what followed

was something she did

that took me by surprise

as she sprinkled water over the leaves

with a bottle of mineral water

as if she had told a lie

and was trying to cover more lies

with another lie

好奇的孩子

"妈妈，什么是野女人呀"
"野女人就是野鸡"

"是不是上次爸爸带
我们去吃的那种鸡呀"

"爸爸吃了，我们也吃了
你为什么生气呀"

"我长大了也要
养一只给妈妈吃"

The Curious Child

'mum, what does "a wild woman" mean?'
'wild women are wild chicks'

'is that the chicken
dad took us to that we ate last time?'

'dad ate it and we ate it, too
but why are you upset'

'when I grow up
I'll raise one for Mum to eat'

情人节

没有约会
没有红包
没有鲜花

这一天
去煌上煌
买了个猪蹄
自己犒赏自己
自己给自己加油
对着光溜溜的蹄子

说——
我爱你

Valentine's Day

no dating

no red packets

no flowers

on this Valentine's Day

I went to Huangshanghuang

and bought a couple of pig's trotters

to reward myself

and to add oil to myself

on top of saying—

to the naked trotters:

I love you

土坯房

这房子
冬暖夏凉
住起来舒服
说这话时
他好像要用
自己的别墅
和它对换

这房子
由泥巴和稻草
构成，风格独特
有自然的气息
有田野的味道
他热烈地赞美
一味地抒情
好像要用
这一身的奢华
换取过去的贫穷

这房子
作为文物和景点
可以用来吸引游客
他终于回到正题
说出了一个商人
真实的想法……

A Mud House

this house
is warm in winter and cool in summer
comfortable to live in
when he said this
he sounded as if he'd swap his villa
with it

this house
built of
mud and rice stock, in a unique style
with breaths of nature
and a taste of the fields
he sang a passionate praise of it
waxing so lyrical
it was almost as if he would
swap his full-bodied luxury
with the past poverty

this house
as a cultural relic and a scenic spot
could be used to attract the tourists
he ended up returning to the main subject

voicing the real thoughts

of a businessman...

憋

憋住不说
就是修养
憋住不拉
就会憋死

憋住
就伟大
憋不住
就出洋相

憋住
满目青山
憋不住
就山洪爆发

憋住
进天堂
憋不住
就下地狱

他憋了一天
还是说了一句
——我好难受

Holding

holding your tongue
that's good manners
holding your poo in
you'll die from it

holding back or in
that's a sign of greatness
not holding back or in
you'll make a fool of yourself

holding back or in
your eyes are full of green hills
not holding back or in
a flood will rush down the mountain

holding back or in
you'll go to heaven
not holding back or in
you'll go to hell

he's been holding back for a whole day

before he finally came out with

—but I'm feeling so awful

真假王小丽

年龄,学历
档案里所有的
公章都是假的
以至于
丈夫,儿子
所有的讲话
都是假的
据说, 只有
性别是真的
通往权力的
阴道是真的
又据说
处女膜
是真的

The True or False Wang Xiaoli

false are all the seals

in her file

as are her age and her academic qualifications

so much so that

whatever her husband

or her son said

was all false

it is said that only

her gender is true

and the vagina to power

is true

but then again it is said that

her maidenhead

is also true

爬山虎

不是东北虎
也不是华南虎
更不是孟加拉虎
是一只绿毛虎
一只无脚爬山虎
它徒有虎名
没有虎威
爬是它的本领
爬是它的绝技
它向仰慕者
炫耀爬的技能
一生都在向上爬
低三而下四
以致得了软骨病
等爬到了顶端
再也直不起腰来
再也抬不起双眼
双手枯瘦向四周伸展
它只享受爬的快乐

The Mountain-Climbing Tiger

is not a Dongbei tiger

nor a Huanan tiger

least of all a Bengal tiger

it is a green-haired tiger

a footless mountain-climbing tiger

with a vain name

but without the powers of a tiger

its forte being its ability to climb

a unique skill

it shows it off

to its admirers

how it's been climbing all its life

degrading itself to such a degree

that it's got a condition of soft bones

when it reaches the top

it can no longer straighten up

nor lift its own eyes

its scrawny hands spreading in all directions

and enjoying alone the pleasure of climbing

Poets's note—1. Mountain-climbing tigers are a reference to an ivy or creeper; 2. Dongbei: northeast China; 3. Huanan: South China.

极端方式

有人把车停在他的车位
他把人家的车给砸了
人家说了他几句
他把人家脑袋砸了
类似这种事还有不少

昨天晚上他突然死了
小区里很多人不相信
——怎么回事啊，这人
还是这种火爆脾气
对别人狠，对自己更狠

据说他的生活
就是这样打和　砸出来的

An Extreme Way

when someone parked his car in his parking place
he smashed the car
when someone said a few things criticising him
he smashed his head
there had been quite a few things like this

last night he suddenly died
stunning many into disbelief in the neighbourhood
—what happened? Why is this guy
so fiery-tempered
fierce to others, fiercer to himself

they say that his life
has been formed by striking   and smashing like this

秋天寄给我的明信片依然是一片红叶

每年十月第一个星期日
她都会给我寄来一张明信片
没有字，没有祝福的语言
什么都没有。空白的地方
任你想象成爱，或者暧昧
而我一如既往地把这片红叶
做成书签夹在某一本诗集
一个季节和它暗藏的秘密
就这样和诗联成一体……

The Postcard, Sent from the Autumn, Remains a Red Leaf

first Sunday every October
she'll send me a postcard
no words, no blessings
nothing. You could imagine
the blank spaces as love or ambiguities
but I, like before, always use this red leaf
as a bookmark in a poetry book
hence a season and its hidden secrets
that are connected with the poems...

过生日

这一天是我的生日
菩萨不知道
住持也不知道
周围的人更不知道
就是知道这事
也跟他们没啥关系
在这庙里
我不烧香
也不点蜡烛
只在心里祈愿
接下来的日子
能够像菩萨一样——
对人世，睁一只眼
闭上另一只眼
整天一言不发
而脸上看起来
还总是
乐乐呵呵

Celebrating My Birthday

it's my birthday today
that Buddha does not know
the head monk doesn't know
and people around me do not know
even if they all know
it's got nothing to do with them
in this temple
I do not burn the incense sticks
nor do I light a candle
all I do is wish at heart
that, in the days to come
I could live like Buddha—
open one eye and close the other
towards the world
keeping mum all day
with a face that seems
always
smiling

人民

他执着的誓言
是为人民服务

他的人民
是妻子儿子
和不同的情妇

今天在被告席上
人民站在对面

People

he persistently vows
to serve the people

his people
are his wife and son
and his various mistresses

today, on the defendant's seat
people stand on the opposite side

逝去的，永恒的……

我的青春在45岁那年嘎然而止
现在它只停留在我的诗里
每当想起那飞扬的生命和情欲
那火焰到今晚还没有黯淡下去
那些日子有时还会回到身边
但远去的背影没有平行的可能
逝去的，永恒的……
都将是一块墓碑

Things That Are Gone and That Are Eternal...

my youth stopped, on a sudden, at 45

it now remains only in my poetry

whenever I recall the flying life and desire

and the fire that remains undarkened even by tonight

those days may sometimes return

although there is no possibility of walking side by side with the person

    who's turned her back

things that are gone and that are eternal...

will be the gravestones

点赞

敬爱的祖母大人昨晚11时10分仙逝
终年91岁，所有儿孙表示沉重哀悼！

这讣告一出
居然有人——点赞

——点你妈的赞
主人狠狠地骂了一句
但他保持了绅士风度，没有骂出声来

Likes

my most beloved Grandmother passed away at 11.10 last night
aged 91, to whom all her children and grandchildren send their deepest
condolences

as soon as the obituary was out
someone clicked 'Like'

fuck the 'Liker'
the one who posted the message kept his gentlemanly manners
short of blurting it out

废弃的矿 洞

洞口的芦苇
长了白发

我只是远远地看着——
幽深，荒芜，孤寂
不可知的过往

火红的岁月
一个又一个男人
他的付出，激情
和无言的叹息

一条富矿的残渣
分钱不值

安民告示提醒你
曾经的喧嚣和热闹

An Abandoned Mine   Cave

the rushes around the mouth of the cave
have turned grey

I stand in the distance, looking—
deep, barren and solitary
with an unknown past

in those fire-red days
man after man
paid his passion
and his wordless sighs

the residue of a rich ore
is worth nothing now

a public notice warns you
about the past hustle and bustle

一个女大学生的初恋

在出租屋里
警察把他按倒在地
戴上手铐
瞬间的变故
让她脑袋"嗡"的一声——
脖子上的金项链
发出凄厉尖叫
每个月的零花钱
血腥四溅
"大叔"不是老板么
不是一家医院的股东么
那么好的一个人
怎么会是……?
她不愿把抢劫犯
安在他的头上——
刚刚给她过完20岁生日
玫瑰花还沾满了露水
上星期还一起去了厦门
鼓浪屿的琴声犹在耳边
"我喜欢你,只想对你好"

这句话好像昨晚说的⋯⋯
眼前是这样虚幻
但他又是那么真实——
他说过，农村老家还有
三个孩子和年迈的父母
看守所里他对警官说
她是无辜的，别告诉学校
别让她父母知道我们的事

First Love of a University Girl Student

in a rented place
the police pinned him to the floor
and handcuffed him
this sudden change
caused her head to go bang—
the gold chain around her neck
shrieked forlornly
as her monthly pocket money
went splashing in blood
wasn't the 'Uncle' the boss of a business
a shareholder of a hospital?
how could such a kind man
have become...?
she did not want to place the title
of a robber on his head—
she had just celebrated her 20th birthday
the roses still stained with dew
only last week they had gone together to Xiamen
the piano still ringing in her ears
'I like you and I want to be good to you alone'
he seemed to have said that only yesterday...
everything in front of her was so unreal
but he was so real—

he had told her that he had three kids

and aged parents at his old home in a village

in the detention centre he said to the police officer

that she was innocent and he told them not to tell her school

not to tell her parents about what had happened between them

且慢

一次急切的表态
有人狠狠地蹦出两字
——且慢。挥手之间
他落下口吃的毛病
慢，不再是动词
也不再是形容词
是一只蜗牛
一生的行为准则
从二十岁到六十岁
在一个黄昏，他
拉下人生的帷幕
彻底慢了下来
无声无息……

Slow Down Please

in a hurried expression of his attitude
someone blurted out in three words:
slow down please. In the waving of a hand
he had become a stutterer
slow, no longer a verb
nor an adjective
was now a snail
his code of conduct for life
from twenty to sixty
on an evening, he
dropped the curtain on his life
perfectly slowed down
in silence...

小职员

"这一生
鄙人有三大爱好
打牌，赢的时候多
输的时候少。嘿嘿，
多数时候还是运气好！
——我很简单，不像你
知识分子，想那么多
还写什么什么狗屁诗
我喜欢喝酒喝酒之后
玩女人，'双飞'那种游戏
刺激！超级棒！现在不行
'飞'不上去！一个还行…"
今天他又有些喝高了
急于表达，脸憋得通红
——这辈子当个小职员
——嘿嘿，也值！

An Office Worker

'all my life
I have loved three things
playing cards, where I win more
than lose. Hey, hey
most of the times, I am lucky!
—I'm a simple man, unlike you
an intellectual; you think too much
and write fucking poetry
I like drinking and playing around with women
after drinking, I play the game of double-flying
that gives me a kick. It doesn't work now
as I can't fly high any more, except with one…'
he's getting drunk and high again today
eager to express himself, his face flushed red
—a small office worker all my life
—and, hey, hey, it's worth it!

唇

一

用酒点燃
并且以爱的名义
这悲哀的四月呵
桃花凋谢在寺庙的屋檐下
在尘世，我只是个偶然的过客
一不小心把春天踩在脚下

二

芦苇在芦苇的岸边
伊人在伊人的水边
秋天的影子还很遥远
用舌尖亲吻舌尖
受伤的是牙齿

The Lips

A

to light up with alcohol
and in the name of love
ah, in this sad April
when peach flowers fade under the eaves of a temple
in this world of dust, I am an accidental passer-by
and I happen to tread the spring underfoot

B

the rushes on the bank of the rushes
and she at the edge of her waters
the shadows of an autumn still far away
and when you kiss the tip of a tongue with the tip of a tongue
it is the teeth that get hurt

阿兰

阿兰是个苦命的女人

阿兰长得很漂亮

是乡村夜空中

最亮最靓的一颗星

十八岁嫁给第一个男人

二十一岁有了第二段婚姻

二十五岁来到城里

她的三个孩子

有四个爹

现在同居的男人

怀疑她

肚子里的孩子

是别人的

阿兰今年三十五岁

据说还有几天就是

她的生日……

Ah Lan

Ah Lan is a woman of a bitter fate
Ah Lan is pretty
the brightest and prettiest star
in the night sky over the village
she married her first man at 18
had her second marriage at 21
and, at 25, she came to the city
but her three kids
had four dads
the man now living with her
suspects that
the child she's pregnant with
is someone else's
Ah Lan is 35 years old this year
they say that it's her birthday
in a few days...

一棵想飞的树

斜着身子

想飞

也曾借助风力

但,泥土

把它拽得很紧

当一只巨鸟

从它的体内飞出

它吓得

不停地抖动

A Tree That Is Thinking of Flying

lying aslant

it thinks of flying

and it did once, on the strength of the wind

although the soil

was tightly dragging it down

when an enormous bird

flew from its inside

it was so scared

it kept trembling

回头

看到无限风光
看到死亡阴影
看到一只蚂蚁
往上爬的曲折与艰险
看到有人踩着
自己的影子坠入深渊
看到别人悲哀的一生
也看到自己
丑陋的一面

When the Head is Turned

one sees a limitless landscape

the shadow of death

the tortuous hardship

of an ant

climbing upwards

someone treading

one's own shadow as he falls into the abyss

someone's sad life in its entirety

and seeing one's own

ugly side

李家庙

小庙修葺一新
菩萨法相庄严
朝拜的人越来越多
香火飘到很远的地方
都说这小庙很灵——
四嫂的心病好了
信财的媳妇怀上了
牛牛又发了……
但根根却在心里嘀咕——
灵个屁，我也拜了好多次
每次打牌都输……

The Li-Family Temple

the small temple looks fresh after the renovation
and the facial features of Buddha are solemn
more and more visitors come
as the smell of incense drifts far and wide
all saying how much this temple works—
fourth sister-in-law, sick at heart, is now cured
daughter-in-law who believes in money has become pregnant
and Niu Niu has made a fortune...
however, Gen Gen is muttering to himself—
it's all hot air, nothing's working, as I've prayed so many times
but I lose at every card game...

分手费的计算方法与结果

她要嫁给他

他始终不答应

两个都有家庭的人

只好坐下来商谈如何分手

——好聚好散当然可以

但必须给我补偿

可怜的男人以沉默

应对着某种尴尬——

说吧，怎么补怎么偿？

——我们在一起10年5个月

零24天，每年一万块钱……

又是沉默，又是争吵

间或还有肢体的冲突

说吧，你说多少吧

男人满是心酸和无奈

——10万5千块，这钱

必须明天上午给我

女人快速地算出结果

并拿出了处理办法

之后他们黯然离开

我也关掉电灯
作为调解人和旁观者
我只想说——
这真他妈的有意思透了！

How to Calculate the Cost of Company-Parting and the Result

she wanted to marry him

but he never agreed

both of them already married

they had to sit down and discuss how to part company

—it would of course be okay to do so amicably

but I have to be somehow compensated

the pitiable man tried to cope with the embarrassment

in silence—

tell me how to compen you and how to sate you?

—we've been together for 10 years, 5 months

and 24 days, 10,000 yuan per year...

amidst silences and fights

with occasional physical altercations

say how much, just say it

the man, feeling sad, was helpless

—15,000 yuan and you must give me

the money tomorrow morning

the woman quickly worked it all out

and produced her way of settlement

afterwards, they left in dejection

and I turned the light off

as a mediator and an onlooker

all I wanted to say—

is this is so fucking interesting!

画框里的蚂蚁

在一片大好河山
它是一个被忽视的对象
意外死亡并成为风景的一部分
它的形象被无限地放大
在玻璃上赤裸裸行走
在光影中展示美的部分
伴随惶恐与不安
我担心有一天
它从画框里走出来
生前默默与身后喧闹
人群里七嘴八舌——
一只画框里的蚂蚁
应该入土为安……

An Ant in the Picture Frame

in a great landscape

it is something ignored

its accidental death having become part of the landscape

and its image enlarged limitlessly

it's walking naked on the glass

revealing its beautiful part in the light and shadow

accompanied with panic and restlessness

I worry that some day

it might walk out of the frame

its silence in life and posthumous commotion

is what people are talking about with seven mouths and eight tongues—

an ant in the picture frame

ought to have been living peacefully in the earth...

短章

哎哟

哎哟，哎……

——这是午夜两点最隐秘的叫喊

——它打破了这个县城的安宁与秩序

她的脊背汗水涔涔

他的手心握住一片波浪

A Short Chapter

aiyo

aiyo, ai...

—that is the most secret cry after 2 a.m.

—and it broke the peace and quiet of this county town

her back was dripping with sweat

and he was holding a wave in the heart of his hand

晚景

落日比我先到

比我更早知道

一根甘蔗的甜和苦

一片甘蔗林的有序和混乱

她嘱我写一首诗

我写下落日的晚景

一个老人在甘蔗地里

弯曲着的背影

我写下老人的子女

个个远走高飞的哨音

我写下晚风吹过

黑夜来临……

An Evening Scene

the setting sun had arrived before me
and it had known earlier than me
the sweet or bitter taste of a sugar cane
and the order or confusion of a sugarcane grove
she asked me to write a poem
so I wrote about the evening scene in which the sun set
and about the bent back
of an old man in the sugarcane grove
I wrote about the old man's kids
and the whistling of their far flight
and I wrote about the arrival of the dark night
as the evening wind blew past...

锈迹之河

铆锈了
船烂了
河流
不撒野了
远行的人
也回不来了
只有
打渔的人
还在梦中
补网
在媳妇怀里
撒欢

A River of Rusty Traces

the anchor has gone rusty

the boat has rotten through

and the river

is no longer wild

the one who's gone away

won't ever come back

only

the fisherman

is still patching his net up

in his dream

and frolicking

in the arms of his wife

大觉山瀑布

"一个人只有一种命运"
向死而生的决心
产生于瞬间
断崖前纵身一跃
不是跌落
尖锐的浪花
内心持续呐喊
是一群石头
撞击虚空
悲哀写下
雄浑的诗篇
伤痛不再抬头

The Cascade on the Dajueshan Mountain

'one individual has only one fate in his life'

the determination to live in the face of death

is born in an instant

when it leaps before the cliff

it's not a fall

the sharp waves

a continuum of inner cries

is a crowd of stones

hitting the vacuum of the skies

as sadness writes down

the vigor of poetry

till the hurt does not raise its head

玻璃房

1
气球飘起来的时候
我正在玻璃房里张望
一只鹰，一只鹰
在我的镜头里像鸟一样

2
其实人要飞起来也很容易
只要给自己安上两只或三只翅膀
只要借助同向的一阵旋风

一只风筝
在飘啊，飘
它多像我曾经的梦魇

3
玻璃有无限的光芒
也有无底的黑暗
我最接近的恰恰是被隐瞒的部分

一只苍蝇闯入
需要足够的勇气
它的盲目总让我哑然

4
能量聚集太多
会让人迅速膨胀
蒸笼里的青蛙
感觉不到死亡的逼近
打开窗户
玻璃中有我的幻影

5
污渍
是一种顽疾
我以病态的目光
注视着变幻的四季
和一轮明月

玻璃之上
有种种可能和诡异风景
天狼星就是最亮的那颗星
它就是玻璃们供奉的皇帝

6

玻璃有两种想法
一种是把心中块垒抹平
并用青藤搭好一架云梯
一种是怀揣一把刀子
必要时可以防身

7

玻璃房是不同玻璃的相加
是生老病死的总和

相同的玻璃涂上不同的颜色
约等于玻璃人戴上不同的面具

8

在冬天
我能感到玻璃的温暖
我能感知玻璃的柔软
玻璃中
有一个广阔的海洋

9

风，找不到出口

正如我在南方找不到北
我在玻璃中找不到东和西

10
玻璃
以威权的傲慢藐视上帝
以尖锐的内心睥睨一切
我在白天看见阳光的黑影
我在深夜看见阴谋和交易
心与心，隔着一层玻璃

11
我在玻璃房种上玫瑰和辣椒
玫瑰是我对生活的向往
辣椒有着火爆的脾气
它们一个长在体内
一个长在体外

12
玻璃房的植物缺氧
玫瑰长成了月季
辣椒戴着茄子的面具

257

它们都有一个扭曲的灵魂
一身讨好主子的毛病

13
爱情是一场游戏
游戏没有规则
玻璃是一面镜子
镜子一碰就碎
无数小镜子
照见不堪的她她她
也照见丑陋的他他他

14
玻璃房没有风雨
阳光也经过过滤
燥热是一种通病
长颈鹿把脖子伸出去
夜夜做着相同的梦

15
我有冷热病
我有偏头痛

我的健忘症来得很突然
它让我与这个世界
保持了适度的距离
玻璃房给了我
——恍惚的人生

The Glasshouse

1

when the balloon went floating up
I was watching in a glasshouse
an eagle, an eagle
was like a bird in my lens

2

it would be easy for a man to fly, as a matter of fact
if he could fix two to three wings onto himself
and if he could rely on a wind whirling in the same direction

a kite
was drifting, drifting
so much like the nightmare I once had

3

the glass had limitless light
and bottomless darkness
but I was closest to the part that was hidden

a fly would have required enough courage
to storm in
its blindness often striking me dumb

4

when too much energy was gathered in one
he would rapidly expand
a frog in a bamboo steamer
could not feel the approach of death
when the window was opened
there was my shadow in the glass

5

stains
are an obstinate disease
with sick eyes, I
watch the changing seasons
and a bright moon

on the glass
there are possibilities and an eerie landscape
the Sky Wolf is the brightest star
an emperor worshipped by the glasses

6

the glass has two thoughts
one that it wants to iron out heaps in the heart
and put up a ladder of cloud with the green ivy
and the other that it wants to carry a knife
in case something happens

7

a glasshouse is a put-together of different glasses
the sum-total of birth, age, sickness and death

similar glasses, painted in different colours
are roughly equal to the different masks that one wears

8

in the winter
I can feel the warmth of the glass
and I can sense the softness of it
inside the glass
there is a vast sea

9

the wind is unable to find an exit
the same way I can't find the north in the south
nor can I find the east and the west in the glass

10

the glass
is contemptuous of God with its authority
and holds everything in contempt with a sharp heart

by day I see the dark shadows of the sun

and by deep night I see conspiracies and transactions
a glass between heart and heart

11

I grow roses and hot chillies in the glasshouse
and the roses are my aspirations for life
the chillies have a fiery temper
one growing on the inside
and the other, on the outside

12

the plants in the glasshouse lack oxygen
and, as a result, roses turn into *yueji*, or China roses
and chillies wear the masks of an eggplant
all with twisted souls
ill with ingratiation

13

love is a game
with no rules
the same way the glass is a mirror

that shatters on contact
countless tiny mirrors
reflecting the helpless her, her and her
and the ugly him, him and him

14

the glasshouse sees no wind and rain

even the sunlight is filtered

the dry heat is a common disease

the giraffe puts out its neck

dreaming the same dream night after night

15

I have a condition in which I go alternately hot and cold

I have migraine

I have a sudden attack of amnesia

that keeps a proper distance

between this world and I

the glasshouse has given me

—a trance-like life

蹲在路边吃盒饭的那个人

盒饭，便宜一点的
三块钱一盒：有豆芽，榨菜
辣椒炒肉（只见辣椒不见肉）
也有五块的……他犹豫了片刻
咬咬牙，还是买了一份贵的
他拿了饭盒，习惯性蹲在路边
他把人行道当成自家的门槛
蹲下来吃，才感觉舒服
这一顿饭，他确实吃得舒服
尤其是那个荷包蛋，值！
瞧他咂嘴巴，一副满意的样子
接着，他从耳夹里
抽出一支烟　点燃
不一会儿，阳关照在他的脸上

The Man Squatting by the Roadside Over His Lunch Box

a lunch box, if cheap

is but 3 yuan a box: Bean sprouts, hot pickled mustard tuber

and pork stir-fried with chili (chili only, no pork)

there are also 5-yuan boxes…he hesitated for a moment,

and, gnawing his teeth, ended up buying a more dear one

with the box of rice, he squatted by the roadside, out of habit

taking the pavement for the threshold of his own house

feeling comfortable eating while squatting

it was such a comforting lunch he had

if only for that poached egg, it was really worth it

now look at him, clicking his tongue, looking pleased

before he took a cigarette

from behind his ear, lighting it

in no time, the sun shone on his face

红汽车

老林在广东打工的女儿回家了
这条刚铺上水泥的小巷
停歇着风光的红汽车
高中毕业，老林的女儿去了广东
她到底干什么没有人知道
有人说她现在是经理秘书
有人说，她担任外商助理
还有人说，她自己开了公司当了老板
手下有几十号人为她跑腿
老林的女儿漂亮、能干
她从小车上拎出大包小包
从小包里拿出大把钞票
老林，一直站在一旁
看着众人，默不作声

The Red Car

Old Lin's daughter who has been working in Guangdong is now back home
this little lane, just paved with cement
is parked with a scenic red car
after she graduated from high school, Old Lin's daughter went to
     Guangdong
though no one knew what she did over there
some say that she's now a secretary working for a manager
some say that she's an assistant to a foreign businessman
and others say that she's the boss, running her own company
with dozens of people running errands for her
Old Lin's daughter is pretty, capable
she is fetching bags, big and small, from the car
and she is taking out bundles of banknotes from her small bag
Old Lin, standing to the side
is watching, not saying a word

寻人启事

我的第N份工作
是拿着小广告到处张贴
像幽灵一样鬼鬼祟祟
像小偷一样躲躲闪闪

把别人的撕掉，或者覆盖
贴上自己的小广告，这时
心情会稍稍放松一些
我会浏览一下周围的事情
——在一张通缉令旁，我
偶然发现一则 寻人启事
竟然写着我的名字
被雨水冲刷的字迹
模糊了我的眼睛

Notice of a Missing Person

my nth job

was to go places and put up small advertisements

sneaking about, like a ghost

evasive, like a thief

removing stuff put up by others or covering them up

with my own and it's not till then

that I felt slightly better

when I could look around and see things

—by the side of a Wanted, I

accidently found one   notice of a missing person

with my name on it

the writing, scourged by the rain

moistened my eyes

像蚂蚁一样

一只又一只行色匆匆的蚂蚁
它们步履艰难而肩负责任
它们面带笑容而表情凝重
它们气喘吁吁而乐此不彼
汗水顺着细小的脸颊流进河里
在晚霞的映衬下熠熠生辉
一只又一只蚂蚁摩肩接踵
向东，或者向西
向南，或者向北
有的背着背囊
有的两手空空
（这是我站在十二层楼顶
所看到的一处风景）

Like the Ants

one ant after another, in a great hurry

struggling along and shouldering responsibilities

smiling but looking dignified

panting but enjoying it

sweat flowing into the river from their tiny faces

shining against the evening glow

one ant after another, rubbing shoulders on the way

to the East, or the West

to the South, or the North

some carrying backpacks

and others empty-handed

(that is a scene I am watching

from the top of a twelve-storey building)

一条高速公路穿过村庄

一条高速公路
把一个村庄分成两半
从此，从村东到村西
需要几个小时
为了交通的便当
有些人，或牲畜
还有些鸟雀
经常横穿公路
就在前几天
又一条发情的狗
倒在高速路的血泊中

A Highway Cutting Through the Village

a highway

cut a village in two

since then, it took several hours

to get from village east to village west

for easy access

some people, or animals

and birds, too

would cross the highway

only a few days ago

another dog in heat

fell in a pool of blood on the highway

酒气中的父亲

在梦里，再一次与你见面
你仍然是一身酒气
一副醉醺醺的样子
那是儿时的记忆，以及
与你最后告别的情景
——在梦里的再现
"酒是好东西，喝一点
既能壮胆，又能御寒"
漂泊旅程的知心朋友
贫寒生活的朴素道理
喝酒。成了你的一种生活
并延续成一种习惯

"酒不是好东西，喝多了
既伤身体，又伤感情"
你醒来说过的话
比酒精挥发得还快
你和酒，是一对生死恋人
我和酒，是天生一对仇敌

在我的记忆里
酒，是母亲的眼泪

Father Smelling of Liquor

in a dream, I see you again

you smell of liquor, like before

looking terribly drunken

memory of my childhood, and

the scene when you last said farewell

—representation in a dream

'liquor is good stuff. When you drink a little

you take guts and keep warm'

a heart-knowing friend on a drifting journey

a simple reason in a destitute life

drinking that has become part of your life

and extends into a habit

'liquor is no good. When you drink too much

it wrecks your health and hurts your feelings'

things you said when you woke up

disappeared faster than the volatilisation of the spirits

you and liquor, a life-and-death couple

while liquor and I, a pair of sworn enemies

in my memory, though

liquor was Mother's tears

老中医

老中医总是斜戴着眼镜

他很少正眼看人，偶尔

看一些患病的部位

比如眼睛，比如舌苔

伤寒、麻疹，各种疑难杂症

只要经他一一把脉

就能找到祖传秘方

他开的方子很简单，也很灵

方圆几十里都知道他的大名

他在老街坐诊几十年

几十年一眨眼就过去了

后来，他的孙子改了招牌

不看中医，只看性病……

The Old Herbal Doctor

the old herbal doctor always wore his glasses askance

he hardly ever looked at people directly in their eyes, except occasionally

when he examined the sick parts

such as the eye or the coating on the tongue

difficult diseases like typhus and measles

would be curable with his secret recipes handed down from his ancestors

once he felt their pulse

his recipe was simple enough, and worked

his name was known for miles around

and he sat in the old street treating people for decades

a passage of time in the twinkling of an eye

subsequently, his grandson has changed his shop sign

no more herbal treatment, as they now only deal with venereal diseases...

旧照片

一张旧照片挂在外婆家的墙上
慈祥的外婆端坐在照片的中央
四世同堂，儿孙绕膝
一个家庭的亲情环绕四周
尊卑有序，长幼相携
一个家庭的幸福写在脸上
时间在那一刻凝固了二十年
外婆的老花镜放大了几十倍
抱在手上的小孙子已经大学毕业
拖着小辫子的外孙女早已做了母亲
旧照片黑白分明，也有点泛黄
照片上有的人看起来有点滑稽
尤其是其中的一个，被抠了眼睛
据说他的眼睛里，阴险地写着
对这个家庭的背叛和仇恨

The Old Photograph

an old photograph is hanging on my granny's wall
my kind granny seated in the centre of the photograph
four generations under one roof, and all her children and grandchildren
encircling her in a family bond
respecting seniority, and the old supporting the young
happiness of a family written on their faces
twenty years, in that moment, frozen in time
amplified a score of times by her presbyopic glasses
the youngest grandson has now graduated from the university
and the granddaughter, with a pigtail, has become a mother
the old photo, in black and white, is yellowing
people in it look a bit funny
particularly one, whose eyes have been scratched off
according to some, betrayal and hatred of the family
were maliciously written in them

村庄的味道

快到家的路上，我闻到了
山坡深处牛嚼青草的味道
草叶深处干牛粪的味道
父亲身上旱烟的味道
一个村庄的味道
在暮色的归途慢慢溢了出来
那里飘着米饭的清香
一粒米饭在煮熟之前
总是昂着高傲的头
而那些红薯的孩子
总是把头埋在地里

The Smells of a Village

on my way nearing home, I smelled

the grass that the cows were chewing in the depths of the hills

the dry cow dung deep in the leaves and grasses

the pipe smoke on my father

and a village

all seeping, slowly, out of my return journey at dusk

the fragrance of cooking rice floating in the air

a drop of rice, before it's cooked

would always keep its head up

while the kids of those sweet potatoes

would keep their heads buried in the soil

5月14日，曹山宝积禅寺

这一天
我看见三种阳光
一株银杏树脸上的阳光
一个小沙弥眼睛里的阳光
一个诗人心灵深处的阳光

银杏树历经千年，死而复生
小沙弥是个穷孩子，孤儿，弃儿
诗人在独自修行的路上

Baoji Buddhist Temple at Caoshan, 14 May

that day
I saw sunlight of three kinds
the sunlight on the face of a gingko tree
the sunlight in the eyes of a young acolyte
and the sunlight in the depths of a poet's heart

the gingko has lived a thousand years, revived from death
the young acolyte is a poor child, an orphan and an abandonee
while the poet is travelling, on the road of solitary practice, Buddhism-wise

睡 莲

钟声在遥远的寺庙响起……

一朵睡莲
在下午醒来
虚度的光阴
是个美梦
众神喧哗
蚂蚁搬家
现在她伸展四肢
在水中
练习瑜伽

The Water Lily

the bell is ringing in the distant temple...

a water lily
wakes up in the afternoon
time wasted
is but a beautiful dream
deities are making a noise
while ants are moving house
now, she extends her limbs
practicing yoga
in the water

鱼和渔翁

只见钓竿
不见渔翁
旁观者担心
鱼上钩以后

一条鱼
突然跃出水面
把问号拉直
又潜入水中

The Fish and the Fisherman

the fishing rod is seen
but not the fisherman
the onlooker is concerned
for the fish when hooked

a fish
suddenly jumps out of the water
stretching the question mark straight
before it dives into the water again

反 差

由一簇乱云
到一场暴雨
到一场灾难发生
几栋民房被毁
泥石流掩埋
几个亡灵
都是在很短时间
发生的事情
一个诗人
在书房写诗
对此浑然不知
他把前面那簇云
写进诗里大加赞美

The Contrast

a cluster of confused clouds

then a rainstorm

that led to a disaster

that destroyed residential houses

and a mudslide

that buried lives

all in quick succession

a poet

writing poetry in his study

was totally unaware of all *that*

he sang praise of the cluster of clouds

into his poetry

五月的稻田

飞起的白鹭
是一种风景
我走在田间
是一种风景
白，黄，绿
三种颜色构成
另一种风景
一头牛，一张犁
一件旧蓑衣
蓝天下的风雨
和雷电
是昨天的风景

Rice Paddies in May

a flying egret
is a windscape
me walking between the rice paddies
is also a windscape
the three colours, white, yellow
and green, are making up
another windscape
while a water buffalo, a ploughshare
an old straw rain cape
the wind and rain in the blue skies
the lightning and the thunder
were yesterday's windscape

巴拿马

这么洋气的名字
是楼下小饭馆的名字
就像一个农村妇女
名字叫玛丽
其实它真的很土气
土鸡，土鸭，土豆
都是土里长的
土鳖，土兔，土拔鼠
一半长在土里
一半长在天上
生意兴隆时
椅子和椅子互相埋怨
来的人不是找不到南
就是找不到北
青菜和茄子互掐
南瓜腆着肚皮傻笑
玛丽只看着客人
客人就是上帝
上帝不能站着

必须搬个小凳子
让他先坐下

Ba Na Ma (Panama)

this, such a foreign one
is the name of the small restaurant downstairs
like the country woman
by the name of Ma Li (Mary)
in fact, it really is earthy
with earthy chickens, earthy ducks and earthy potatoes
all grown up from the earth
and with earthy turtles, earthy rabbits and earthy groundhogs
half grown in the earth
and the other half, in the sky
when business is brisk
chairs and chairs are complaining of each other
because the customers fail to find either the south
or the north
vegetables and eggplants are at each other's throats
while pumpkins laugh a stupid laugh, with bulging bellies
all Ma Li does is look at her customers
because they are her God
and as her God they can't be allowed to stand
she has to pull a stool over
for them to sit down on

www.ingramcontent.com/pod-product-compliance
Lightning Source LLC
Chambersburg PA
CBHW031043110426
42740CB00048B/803